**Harcourt**

# Test Preparation

## Grade 7

ISBN  978-0-544-26859-3

 2 3 4 5 6 7 8 9 10   0982   22 21 20 19 18 17 16 15 14

4500510529      A B C D E F G

Dear Parent or Educator,

Welcome to *Core Skills: Test Preparation*. You have selected a book that will help your child develop the skills he or she needs to succeed on standardized tests.

Although testing can be a source of anxiety for children, this book will give your child the preparation and practice that he or she needs to feel better prepared and more confident when taking a standardized test. Research shows that children who are acquainted with the scoring format of standardized tests score higher on those tests. Students also score higher when they practice and understand the skills and strategies needed to take standardized tests. The subject areas and concepts presented in this book are typically found on standardized tests at this grade level.

To best help your child, please consider the following suggestions:

- Provide a quiet place to work.
- Go over the directions and the sample exercises together.
- Review the strategy tips.
- Reassure your child that the practice tests are not "real" tests.
- Encourage your child to do his or her best.
- Check the lesson when it is complete.
- Go over the answers and note improvements as well as problems.

If your child expresses anxiety about taking a test or completing these lessons, help him or her understand what causes the stress. Then, talk about ways to eliminate anxiety. Above all, enjoy this time you spend with your child. He or she will feel your support, and test scores will improve as success in test taking is experienced.

Help your child maintain a positive attitude about taking a standardized test. Let your child know that each test provides an opportunity to shine.


Sincerely,

The Educators and Staff of
Houghton Mifflin Harcourt


P.S. You might want to visit our website at **www.hmhco.com** for more test preparation materials as well as additional review of content areas.

# Core Skills: Test Preparation

# GRADE 7

## Contents

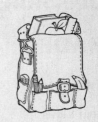

Dear Student,

Sometime during the school year, you will be taking standardized tests. This book can help you prepare to take such tests.

Here are some suggestions for using these practice tests and for taking the "real" tests.

**DO**

- Listen to or read all the directions.
- Read the **Try This** strategy tips, do the **Sample** items, and then look at **Think It Through** to check your answer before you begin each lesson.
- Look over the entire test or section before you begin.
- Stay calm, concentrate on the test, and clear your mind of things that have nothing to do with the test.
- Read all the answer choices before choosing the one that you think is best.
- Make sure the number you fill in on the answer sheet matches the question number on the test page.
- Trust your first instinct when answering each question.
- Answer the easy questions first, then go back and work on the ones you aren't sure about.
- Take all the time you are allowed.

**DON'T**

- Look ahead to another question until you complete the one you're working on.
- Spend too much time on one question.
- Rush.
- Worry if others finish while you are still working.
- Change an answer unless you are really sure it should be changed.

**Remember to do your best!**

# Standardized Test Content Areas

The following skills are tested on most standardized exams. These same skills are included in *Core Skills: Test Preparation, Grade 7*.

## Reading Skills

*Identifying synonyms

*Using sentence context to determine word meaning

*Identifying passage details, the main idea, sequence of events, genre, cause and effect

*Recognizing supporting details

*Making inferences

*Analyzing character

*Drawing conclusions

 Distinguishing between fact and opinion

*Identifying the author's purpose

+Determining tone

 Determining likely source of text

*Using definitional phrases to determine word meanings

## Language Skills

*Determining topic relevance

*Organizing information

*Identifying the correct use of general reference materials

*Interpreting dictionary entries

 Using a table of contents and an index of a book to locate information

*Understanding vocabulary

*Distinguishing between clearly written sentences and those with errors in expression or construction

*Determining appropriate topic sentences and supporting sentences

*Identifying extraneous information within a paragraph

*Identifying correctly applied grammar

*Identifying correct capitalization and punctuation

*Recognizing misspelled words in context

*Identifying correct spellings of words in context

## Mathematics Skills

 Comparing and ordering fractions

 Identifying equivalent fractions and improper fractions

+Identifying alternative decimal representations and number line integers

+Identifying place value of decimals, scientific notation, and powers and square roots

 Distinguishing between primes and composites

 Identifying and evaluating linear expressions

*Solving linear equations and identifying the solution equation to a problem expressed in words

+Finding the output of functions

 Identifying missing elements in number patterns

*Using rate or proportion to solve problems

*Determining combination and permutations and predicting outcomes

*Identifying probabilities

 Reading and interpreting multiple-line graphs, tables, circle graphs, and tally charts

 Determining the mean

 Calculating volume, area of plane figures, and circumference

 Classifying polyhedrons and angles

+Identifying coordinates, radius and diameter, transformations, and parallel and perpendicular lines

 Converting measurement units and determining measurements indirectly from similar figures and scale drawings

 Measuring length and identifying elapsed time

*Using estimation and identifying reasonableness

*Identifying missing information and using problem-solving strategies

*Demonstrating the ability to add, subtract, multiply, and divide

*Applying addition, subtraction, multiplication, and division concepts to word problems

*Aligns to Grade 7 Common Core State Standards.

+Extension: Aligns to Grade 8 Common Core State Standards.

v

# Listening Scripts

These scripts accompany the listening portions of the lessons and tests found in Unit 7 on pages 80–83 and in Unit 12 on pages 118 and 119. Before beginning the test, work the sample question with your child and discuss the correct answer. In all listening lessons and tests, give your child time to respond before reading the next question. You may read these items twice if needed.

## UNIT 7: LISTENING

### Understanding Word Meanings, p. 80

Look at Sample A. I will read a sentence and the four answer choices. You will find the word that best completes the sentence. Listen carefully.

The dog bared its **fangs** at the stranger. **Fangs** are a kind of — **A** fur … **B** eyes … **C** teeth … **D** bones. Darken the circle for the word that best completes the sentence. (Discuss the question and answer as needed.)

Now you will do numbers 1 through 10. Listen carefully to the sentence and the four answer choices. Then darken the circle for the correct answer. For number 10, write your answer in the space provided.

1. The police officer had to **ascertain** the cause of the accident. To ascertain is to — **A** confuse … **B** miss … **C** determine …**D** report.

2. Max's **petty** concerns caused problems for his friends. Something that is petty is — **F** usual … **G** unimportant … **H** worthwhile … **J** serious.

3. The factory was **liable** for injuries to its employees. *Liable* means — **A** closed … **B** unreliable … **C** blameless … **D** responsible.

4. You have to **compute** the total cost of the purchases. To compute is to — **F** calculate … **G** know … **H** grasp … **J** estimate.

5. Congress can **override** a president's veto. To override is to — **A** ratify … **B** uphold … **C** support … **D** cancel.

6. They made sure that the child was not **lagging** behind. *Lagging* means — **F** lingering … **G** hurrying … **H** overtaking … **J** running.

7. Her **impulsive** nature sometimes got her into trouble. *Impulsive* means — **A** not serious … **B** silly … **C** not planned … **D** deliberate.

8. Marissa was met at the airport with a **garland** of flowers. A garland is a kind of — **F** vase … **G** box … **H** wreath … **J** handful.

9. The hospital's nursing staff will **dispense** medication to the patients. *To dispense* means to — **A** gather … **B** collect … **C** retain … **D** distribute.

10. His **valiant** efforts couldn't save the burning house. *Valiant* means — (Your child should write an answer on the blank lines.)

### Building Listening Skills, p. 81

Look at Sample A. I will read a paragraph and then ask a question. You will choose the best answer to the question. Listen carefully.

People who live in different climates build different kinds of houses. In the western United States, where it is very hot, some houses are made of a kind of mud called adobe that keeps the heat out. In cold climates people build houses with sloping roofs so the snow will slide off easily.

People build houses with sloping roofs because they are concerned about the — **A** snow … **B** rain … **C** cold … **D** heat. (Discuss the question and answer as needed.)

Now you will practice answering more questions about passages. Find question 1. Listen carefully to the passage and the question. Then darken the circle for the correct answer. You will answer three questions.

The Hopi Indians lived in the southwest region of the United States in an area we now know as Arizona. They produced most of the things they needed to survive. They made pottery for their dishes, grew cotton that they spun into yarn to make clothing, raised sheep, and grew their own food.

**vi**

1. The Hopi Indians grew cotton to make —
   **A** clothing …**B** tents … **C** paper … **D** blankets.

2. The Hopi Indians raised — **F** cattle …
   **G** sheep …**H** chickens … **J** goats.

3. In which part of the United States did the
   Hopi Indians live? **A** the Pacific Northwest …
   **B** the Southeast …**C** the Northeast …
   **D** the Southwest.

Now find number 4. Listen to this announcement.
You will answer four questions.

Numerous schools in the Southeast were
recently damaged or destroyed by a hurricane.
These schools need help in order to open by the
beginning of October. Our school has adopted
Jackson Junior High School in southern Florida.
We will hold a school-supply drive to help the
students. The supplies needed include gym
bags, locks for lockers, art boxes, scissors, pens
and pencils, folders, rulers, and notebooks. The
drive will begin on Monday, September 4, and
end Friday, September 22. Please bring your
donations to the school gym before or after
school. Students wishing to volunteer to sort
and pack items and label boxes, should contact
the principal.

4. How did the schools in the Southeast get
   damaged? **F** they burned … **G** a hurricane …
   **H** an earthquake … **J** a tornado.

5. The drive will begin — **A** on September 4 …
   **B** on September 22 … **C** in October …
   **D** on September 15.

6. Donations should be brought to —
   **F** individual classrooms … **G** Jackson Junior
   High School … **H** the school gym …
   **J** the principal's office.

7. The author expects that — **A** the drive will not
   be successful … **B** the principal may not
   approve the school-supply drive … **C** the
   students will volunteer to adopt another school
   … **D** Jackson Junior High School will rebuild
   and reopen soon.

Now find number 8. Listen to this paragraph. You
will answer three questions.

Everyone has goals, or hopes and dreams for
the future. Setting goals can be beneficial
because it can help you gain control of your life
and can help you shape your life in a positive
way. Before setting a goal, it is helpful to
decide what your interests are, to determine
what your strengths are, and to know what your
values are. Then use the following steps to help
you set and achieve your goals:

- Work on only one goal at a time.
- Make your goal clear and specific.
- Make a list of things you need to do to
  achieve your goal.
- Get help from others if you need to.
- Set a realistic date to reach your goal.
- Reward yourself when you achieve your goal.

8. Where are you most likely to find this
   paragraph? **F** in a science book …
   **G** in a teen magazine … **H** in a newspaper …
   **J** in a news magazine.

9. To achieve a goal, it is helpful to —
   **A** make the goal specific … **B** have as much
   time as possible … **C** work on several
   goals at a time … **D** try to achieve the goal
   without help.

10. What does the author believe people should
    determine before setting a goal? **F** the time
    available to reach the goal … **G** their interests,
    strengths, and values … **H** who can help with
    achieving the goal … **J** the reward for achieving
    the goal.

## Test, pp. 82–83

(Give your child scratch paper to take notes if needed.)

In this test you will use the listening skills we have practiced in this unit. This test is divided into two parts. For each part there is a sample exercise. Look at Sample A. I will read a sentence and the four answer choices. You will find the word that best completes the sentence. Listen carefully.

Mandy gave us a **hearty** welcome when we returned. *Hearty* means — **A** reluctant … **B** cold … **C** friendly … **D** small. Darken the circle for the word that best completes the sentence.

You should have darkened the circle for C, friendly, because *hearty* means "friendly."

Now find number 1. We will do numbers 1 through 13. Listen carefully to the sentence and the four answer choices. Then darken the circle for the correct answer. For number 13, write your answer in the space provided.

1. Mary's movements were **sluggish** as she finished the dance rehearsal. *Sluggish* means — **A** energetic … **B** slow … **C** precise … **D** jerky.

2. They saw the injured animal **writhe** with pain. To writhe is to — **F** cry … **G** yelp … **H** squirm … **J** suffer.

3. My grandmother was a **shrewd** judge of character. *Shrewd* means — **A** harsh … **B** kind … **C** foolish … **D** clever.

4. The teacher will have to **banish** Ryan from club meetings because of his rowdy behavior. To banish is to — **F** bring in … **G** send away … **H** accept … **J** return.

5. We stood on the dock and watched the **turbulent** sea. *Turbulent* means — **A** gray … **B** calm … **C** silent … **D** stormy.

6. Brad ate an **ample** portion of the pie. *Ample* means — **F** scarce … **G** large … **H** meager … **J** small.

7. Some tribes in the Sahara still lead a **nomadic** existence. *Nomadic* means — **A** wandering … **B** settled … **C** stationary … **D** resident.

8. Some European countries remained **neutral** during World War II. *Neutral* means — **F** involved … **G** biased … **H** uninvolved … **J** subjective.

9. Sheila was satisfied with her **productive** day at the office. *Productive* means — **A** worthwhile … **B** useless … **C** pointless … **D** unprofitable.

10. We enjoyed the **luscious** apples that we picked. *Luscious* means — **F** bitter … **G** tasteless … **H** bland … **J** delicious.

11. Marcie had a **knack** for working with small children. A knack is a — **A** desire … **B** skill … **C** inability … **D** job.

12. Her orange hat made her **conspicuous** in the crowd. *Conspicuous* means — **F** noticeable … **G** invisible … **H** insignificant … **J** subtle.

13. The watch was still **intact** after it fell in the pool. Something that is intact is — (Your child should write an answer on the blank lines.)

Now turn to page 83.

Look at Sample B. I will read a passage and then ask a question. You will choose the best answer to the question. Listen carefully.

> The Maya were Native Americans who lived in Central America. Their civilization flourished from about A.D. 250 to 900. They were skilled astronomers who used astronomy to develop a calendar.

This paragraph would most likely be found in a — **A** hobby magazine … **B** history book … **C** science magazine … **D** psychology book. Darken the circle for the correct answer.

You should have darkened the circle for B, history book, because this kind of information would most likely be found in a history book.

Now find number 14. Listen carefully to the passage and the questions. Then darken the circle for the correct answer. For number 26, write your answer in the space provided. You will answer three questions.

If you eat a healthy, well-balanced diet, you should be getting all the vitamins your body needs from your food. However, since some people skip meals or eat unhealthy foods, they take vitamin pills. Taking vitamin pills is a way to be sure you are getting your minimum daily requirement of vitamins.

14. According to the paragraph, people who eat unhealthy foods — **A** should exercise more … **B** should take vitamin pills … **C** need to learn about nutrition … **D** buy more vitamins than other people.

15. A good title for this paragraph is — **F** "A Good Diet" … **G** "Everyone Needs Vitamins" … **H** "Why Take Vitamin Supplements?" … **J** "Foods to Avoid."

16. The main purpose of this paragraph is — **A** to inform … **B** to persuade … **C** to entertain … **D** to inspire.

Now find number 17. Listen to this passage. You will answer four questions.

John Glenn flew many kinds of planes before he became an astronaut. As a Marine Corps pilot, he flew missions during World War II and the Korean War. Glenn was also a test pilot. In 1957, he flew from Los Angeles to New York City in about three and a half hours. He set a new speed record and made headlines. Glenn was later chosen to work with the Mercury program. This program aimed to put an American into space. On February 20, 1962, John Glenn became the first American to orbit Earth. He orbited Earth three times in just under five hours. Altogether, he traveled 80,966 miles!

17. In what year did John Glenn orbit earth? **F** 1962 … **G** 1964 … **H** 1975 … **J** 1984.

18. John Glenn made headlines when he — **A** set a new speed record … **B** wrote newspaper articles … **C** flew missions during World War II … **D** flew missions during the Korean War.

19. The goal of the Mercury program was to — **F** put an American into space … **G** help Glenn become a hero …**H** train test pilots … **J** win the Korean War.

20. John Glenn was all of the following except — **A** an astronaut … **B** a newspaper reporter … **C** a test pilot … **D** a Marine Corps pilot.

Now find number 21. Listen to this story. You will answer six questions.

My friends always search for summer jobs. Summer is a good time to make money, which will be needed during the school year. Last summer Janet mowed lawns while Luis and I delivered newspapers. Margaret and Joey took care of the children in the neighborhood. Alex got the most exciting job of all. His job was to walk the Clark's huge dog Biff three times a day. Usually all we saw were flashes of Alex and Biff. It seems that Biff loves to chase cats and squirrels. Sometimes it was hard to tell who was in charge of things. As Biff took his daily runs, Alex fought just to hang on!

21. In the story, Biff was — **F** a squirrel … **G** a dog … **H** one of the friends … **J** the writer's little brother.

22. Why did the friends look for summer jobs? **A** to please their parents … **B** to make money … **C** to help their neighbors … **D** to complete a school project.

23. The writer's summer job involved — **F** mowing lawns … **G** taking care of children … **H** walking a dog … **J** delivering newspapers.

24. Why did the people in the story see only flashes of Alex and Biff? **A** Biff ran and pulled Alex with him … **B** Alex did not want people to see them … **C** They took pictures of Alex and Biff … **D** Biff was very shy.

25. Whose summer job did the author think was most exciting? **F** Janet's … **G** Luis's … **H** Joey's … **J** Alex's.

26. A good title for this story is — (Your child should write an answer on the blank lines.)

ix

# UNIT 12: COMPREHENSIVE TEST

## Practice Test 4: Listening, pp. 118–119

(Before you begin, be sure your child is using the bubble-in form on page 128 to record answers. Give your child scratch paper to take notes if needed.)

In this test you will use your reading skills to answer questions. This test is divided into two parts. For each part there is a sample exercise. Look at Sample A. I will read a sentence and the four answer choices. You will find the word that best completes the sentence. Listen carefully.

Dad wanted to **mingle** with the guests at the party. To mingle is to — **A** avoid … **B** concentrate … **C** mix … **D** separate. Darken the circle for the word that best completes the sentence.

You should have darkened the circle for C, mix, because *to mingle* means to "mix."

Now you will do numbers 1 through 17. Listen carefully to the sentence and the four answer choices. Then darken the circle for the correct answer.

1. Is the payment on Penny's bicycle **overdue**? *Overdue* means — **A** completed … **B** late … **C** arrived … **D** recent.

2. Grandmother's daily four-mile walk helps to keep her **robust**. *Robust* means — **F** weak … **G** ill … **H** strong … **J** lonely.

3. The vacationers were **prohibited** from swimming in that area. If something is prohibited, it is — **A** forgiven … **B** encouraged … **C** forbidden … **D** taxed.

4. In the class play, Ben played the part of a **sentry** in a medieval castle. A sentry is a kind of — **F** guard … **G** servant … **H** athlete … **J** clerk.

5. Dr. Martin Luther King, Jr., was a great **orator**. An orator is a skillful — **A** speaker … **B** carpenter … **C** architect … **D** governor.

6. The **rookie** ballplayer made a fantastic play. A rookie is — **F** an expert … **G** a specialist … **H** a veteran … **J** a beginner.

7. Martha **shunned** her mother's advice. To shun something is to — **A** welcome it … **B** ignore it … **C** follow it … **D** include it.

8. Her **prior** interview resulted in a new job. *Prior* means — **F** following … **G** next … **H** previous … **J** effective.

9. We drove down a peaceful, **meandering** road. Something that is meandering is — **A** long … **B** crumbling … **C** winding … **D** straight.

10. It was **imperative** that Mr. Taniguchi went to the meeting. *Imperative* means — **F** necessary … **G** unimportant … **H** optional … **J** intelligent.

11. Harriet's **fortitude** enabled her to climb the mountain. *Fortitude* means — **A** planning … **B** strength … **C** skill … **D** frailty.

**x**

12. The politician **conceded** defeat in the election. *To concede* means to — **F** resist … **G** welcome … **H** deny … **J** acknowledge.

13. In the spring, Rolando was **afflicted** with allergies. *Afflicted* means very — **A** soothed … **B** comforted … **C** bothered … **D** relieved.

14. The soccer club is now **recruiting** new members. *Recruiting* means — **F** releasing … **G** enlisting … **H** rejecting … **J** training.

15. Do you know if the man gave a **fictitious** name to the reporter? Something that is fictitious is — **A** false … **B** humorous … **C** truthful … **D** complete.

16. This is a **contemporary** version of an old design. *Contemporary* means — **F** different … **G** famous … **H** current … **J** beautiful.

17. Brenda had a sense of **foreboding** about her upcoming test. *Foreboding* means — **A** dread … **B** peace … **C** confidence … **D** trust.

Now turn to page 119.

Look at Sample B. I will read a paragraph and then ask a question. You will choose the best answer to the question. Listen carefully.

> Acid rain is a threat to the environment. Acid rain is rain mixed with acidic gases given off when fuels such as coal, gas, or oil burn. Acid rain kills fish and damages crops and forests.

What causes acid rain? **A** gases from burning fuels that mix with rain … **B** heavy rainfall … **C** rain that falls on forests … **D** rain that falls over farms. Darken the circle for the correct answer.

You should have darkened the circle for A, gases from burning fuels that mix with rain. The paragraph states that acid rain is rain mixed with acidic gases given off when fuels burn.

Find number 18. Listen carefully to the passage and the question. Then darken the circle for the correct answer. You will answer four questions.

> In Salisbury, England, you can see a group of large, rough stones placed together thousands of years ago. This ancient monument is called Stonehenge. No one knows why it is there. Some scientists believe it was used as a calendar to predict the seasons and the phases of the moon.

18. Stonehenge is made up of a group of — **F** trees … **G** stones … **H** houses … **J** calendars.

19. Stonehenge might have been used as a — **A** calendar … **B** village … **C** castle … **D** school.

20. Stonehenge is located in — **F** New York … **G** England … **H** Mexico … **J** Holland.

21. A good title for this selection is — **A** "An Ancient Mystery" … **B** "Fun Vacation Spots" … **C** "Understanding Geology" … **D** "The English Calendar."

© Houghton Mifflin Harcourt Publishing Company

Now find number 22. Listen to this passage. You will answer two questions.

There are many varieties of popcorn. Caramel-covered and cheese-flavored popcorn have been available for a number of years. New flavors include nacho, barbecue, and ranch popcorn. In some shopping malls there are stores that sell nothing but gourmet flavored popcorns. Of course, you can still order popcorn with just melted butter — the original flavor!

22. Stores that sell gourmet flavored popcorns are often found in — F other countries … G shopping malls … H large cities … J cold climates.

23. A new flavor of popcorn is — A nacho … B caramel … C cheese … D butter.

Now find number 24. Listen to this passage. You will answer four questions.

Vegetables can be prepared in a variety of ways. You can steam vegetables by placing them in a steamer over simmering water in a covered pan. Some vegetables, such as potatoes, can be baked with their skins on. You need to pierce the skins in order to prevent the vegetables from bursting. You can cut vegetables in pieces and microwave them in an appropriate container. Another tasty way to prepare vegetables is to stir-fry them. This method involves cooking vegetables quickly over high heat in only a small amount of oil.

24. To prevent potatoes from bursting while baking in an oven, you need to — F pierce the skins … G steam them first … H microwave them … J use a small amount of oil.

25. Stir-frying vegetables involves — A placing them in a steamer … B baking them in an oven … C cooking them quickly over high heat … D microwaving them.

26. A good title for this article is — F "A Well-Balanced Diet" … G "Cooking Techniques for Vegetables" … H "Steaming Vegetables" … J "Vegetable Recipes."

27. This article would most likely appear in — A a biology book … B a gardening book … C a plant book … D a cookbook.

Now find number 28. Listen to this announcement. You will answer three questions.

Help us get ready for the Stevenson Junior High School "block party" sponsored by Stevenson's PTA. This is a school-wide party, which will be held on the school grounds. It will take the place of end-of-the-year individual class parties. The block party will be held on May 30th from 12:30 P.M. to 3:15 P.M. We are planning to have refreshments, games, and music by a high school rock band. We need volunteers to work on the refreshment committee, the game committee, and the clean-up committee. Please use the sign-up lists in the office to indicate the committee you want to work with. Sign up by April 30th.

28. All of the following will be included in the block party except — F refreshments … G games … H contests … J music.

29. You can sign up for one of the party committees — A in the auditorium … B in the school office … C in your classroom … D at a PTA meeting.

30. When will the block party take place? F on May 30th … G on the last day of school … H in the morning … J on April 30th.

# Core Skills: Test Preparation

# INTRODUCTION

Standardized tests are becoming increasingly more important in both public and private schools, yet test anxiety causes many children to perform below their fullest potential. *Core Skills: Test Preparation* is designed to help children succeed on standardized tests. This program refreshes basic skills, familiarizes children with test formats and directions, and teaches test-taking strategies.

A large part of being well prepared for a test is knowing how to approach different types of questions and learning how to use time wisely. *Core Skills: Test Preparation* gives children the opportunity to take a test under conditions that parallel those they will face when taking standardized tests. This practice and experience will allow them to feel more confident when taking standardized tests and will enable them to demonstrate their knowledge successfully.

## Tools for Success

*Core Skills: Test Preparation* gives children valuable practice with the content areas and question formats of the major standardized tests used nationally.

*Core Skills: Test Preparation* provides the following:
- Test-taking strategies
- Familiarity with test directions
- Review of skills and content
- Awareness of test formats
- Practice tests

## Organization

The book is divided into units that correspond to those found on standardized tests.

- Reading Comprehension
- Reading Vocabulary
- Mathematics Problem Solving
- Mathematics Procedures
- Listening
- Language

*Core Skills: Test Preparation* is designed to ensure success on test day by offering the following:

### Strategies for Taking Reading Tests
Unit 1 provides valuable test-taking strategies that help children do their best on the reading portion of any standardized test.

### Targeted Reading Objectives
Unit 2 focuses on six reading objectives. Each practice question includes a hint to help your child master the targeted objective.

### Strategies for Solving Math Problems
Unit 5 offers a step-by-step approach to solving word problems.

## Skill Lessons

Units 3, 4, 6, 7, and 8 prepare your child by providing both content review and test-taking strategies. Each skill lesson includes the following:

*Directions*—state test instructions clearly, concisely, and in a format similar to that of standardized tests

*Try This*—offers a test strategy that helps children approach each question in a logical way

A *Sample*—familiarizes children with the "look and feel" of test items

*Think It Through*—specifically explains the correct answer to the Sample question

A *Practice Section*—contains a set of practice items that are focused on a specific skill and modeled on items from standardized tests

A *Unit Test*—covers all the skills in the lessons

## Practice Tests

Units 9–13 simulate the content and format your child will encounter when taking standardized tests in reading comprehension, vocabulary, math, listening, and language.

**1**

# Using This Book

### *Try This* and *Think It Through*

The *Try This* and *Think It Through* features accompany the sample questions on the skill lesson pages. Before your child answers the sample question, read the *Try This* skill strategy aloud. Give your child time to answer the question, and then review the correct answer using the information in *Think It Through*.

### Answering the Questions

*Answer Bubbles*—Show your child how to fill in the multiple choice bubble-in answers. Stress the importance of filling the answer bubble completely, pressing firmly with the pencil, and erasing any stray marks. On the skill lesson pages, the answer bubbles are next to the answer choices. For the six practice tests, your child will use the bubble-in *Answer Sheet for Students* on pages 127–128.

*Short Answer Questions*—Standardized tests also require children to write the answers to some questions. *Core Skills: Test Preparation* gives children practice answering this type of question. Students should answer short answer, or open-ended, questions on a separate sheet of paper.

### Scripts for Listening Tests

The lessons and tests in Unit 7 (pages 80–83) and Unit 12 (pages 118–119) require that an adult read a scripted text while the child answers the questions. These scripts are collected in the section titled *Listening Scripts* on pages vi–xii. The pages are perforated so that you can remove them easily. This way, your child can mark the answers in the book while you read from the loose pages.

### Practice Tests

The six practice tests, pages 96–126, simulate standardized tests, providing your child with valuable practice before test day. Like many standardized tests, these are timed. The following are the suggested times needed to administer each test:

| | |
|---|---|
| Reading Comprehension | 35 minutes |
| Reading Vocabulary | 20 minutes |
| Math Problem Solving | 50 minutes |
| Math Procedures | 15 minutes |
| Listening | 25 minutes |
| Language | 35 minutes |

### Answer Sheet for Students

On pages 127–128, you will find a bubble-in answer sheet very similar to the type of form your child will use during a standardized test. Your child will use this blank form to answer the six practice tests. If you think your child might want to repeat a test, be sure to copy the blank form *before* your child uses it.

### Answer Key

A complete answer key begins on page 129. The pages are perforated so that you can remove them easily and return the book to your child. Note that pages 131–132 are a bubble-in form with the correct answers already entered. Do not confuse these pages with the blank Answer Sheet for Students on pages 127–128.

## Icons

This book contains the following icons to help you and your child:

 The **Go On** icon tells your child that the test continues on the next page.

 The **Stop** icon tells your child to stop working.

 The **Listen** icon tells you and your child that it is time to work together. Turn to the *Listening Scripts* section (pages vi–xii) to locate the script you need.

 The stopwatch icon indicates the amount of time to allot for each **Practice Test**.

The lessons and practice tests in *Core Skills: Test Preparation* provide children with the tools they need to build self-confidence. That self-confidence can translate into a positive test-taking experience and higher scores on standardized tests. With its emphasis on skills, strategies for success, and practice, *Core Skills: Test Preparation* gives children the ability to succeed on standardized tests.

# Unit 1: Reading Test-Taking Strategies

The following strategies will help you do your best on standardized reading tests. These three strategies will assist you in organizing the information needed to successfully answer the questions.

## STRATEGY 1
### The Check and See Strategy

This strategy can be used when a question asks for a fact from the passage. The answer to the question is right there in the passage. It is not hidden. Some of the same words may be in the passage and in the question.

 **Check and See** will help you answer *remembering information* questions.

---

**This is the Check and See Strategy**

1. **READ: Read** the question.

2. **FIND: Find** the words you need in the passage.

3. **DECIDE: Decide** which strategy to use.
   **Check and See:** Put a **check** next to the sentence where you can **see** the words you need to answer the question.

4. **ANSWER:** Choose the best **answer.**

---

# STRATEGY 2
## The Puzzle Piece Strategy

This strategy can be used when a question asks you what something means. Sometimes there does not seem to be an answer. It is not stated in the passage.

 **Puzzle Piece** is the strategy to use when you must fit facts together to get the answer. This is like putting a puzzle together. Puzzles are made up of many pieces. You cannot look at one piece and know what the picture is. Only when you put the pieces together can you see the whole picture.

**This is the Puzzle Piece Strategy**

1. **READ: Read** the question.

2. **FIND: Find** the facts you need in the passage.

3. **DECIDE: Decide** which strategy to use.
    **Write: Write** the facts in puzzle pieces.
    **Put Together: Put** the puzzle pieces **together** to see the picture.

4. **ANSWER:** Choose the best **answer.**

## STRATEGY 3
### The What Lights Up Strategy

This is another strategy you can use when an answer is not in the passage. To answer the question you need to add your own ideas to the passage. This added information can come from your own experiences.

 **What Lights Up** can help you see if something is true, real, useful, or a fact. It can help you see what would happen if the story had a different ending.

You can use the **What Lights Up Strategy** to answer the hardest type of question. This is when you are asked to read and think of your own ideas. These questions are called *evaluating* and *extending meaning* questions.

**This is the What Lights Up Strategy**

1. **READ: Read** the question.

2. **FIND: Find** the facts you need in the passage.

3. **DECIDE: Decide** which strategy to use.
   **Write: Write** the facts in the book.
   **Think: Think** about your own ideas.
   **Light Up:** Think about what you have written.
   The answer will **light up** in your mind.

4. **ANSWER:** Choose the best **answer.**

Core Skills Test Prep, Grade 7

# Unit 2: Reading Comprehension

## SPECIFIC OBJECTIVES

**Objective 1:**     **Determining word meanings**
Prefixes and suffixes, context clues, technical words, and words
with multiple meanings

**Objective 2:**     **Identifying supporting ideas**
Recalling facts and details, sequential order, following
directions, and describing settings

**Objective 3:**     **Summarizing main ideas**
Stated and implied main ideas, and identifying summaries

**Objective 4:**     **Perceiving relationships and recognizing outcomes**
Cause-and-effect and making predictions

**Objective 5:**     **Making inferences and generalizations**
Interpreting graphs and diagrams, inferring information,
drawing conclusions, making judgments, and evaluating plot

**Objective 6:**     **Recognizing points of view, facts, and opinions**
Author's purpose, persuasive language, and discerning facts and
points of view

Name _____ Date _____

**Directions: Read each passage carefully. Darken the circle for the correct answer, or write your answer in the space provided.**

# OBJECTIVE 1: DETERMINING WORD MEANINGS

Prefixes and suffixes are parts of some words. A *prefix* appears at the beginning of a word. A *suffix* appears at the end of a word. Both prefixes and suffixes affect the meaning of the word. You can use them to help figure out the meaning of a word.

Both of the teenagers had a problem with their mother. They were good students, helped around the house, and did their own laundry. But she remained hypercritical.

1. In this selection, the word hypercritical means —

   Ⓐ hysterical.

   Ⓑ underactive.

   Ⓒ overly critical.

   Ⓓ under pressure.

   *Hint: "Hyper-" is a prefix that means* too much.

Bob went to look at the apartment with the realtor. The neighborhood looked nice enough, and there were lots of stores within walking distance. They walked up a flight of stairs outside; it was the first apartment on the right. When they opened the door, Bob could not believe how spacious the rooms were.

2. In this paragraph, the word spacious means —

   Ⓕ large.

   Ⓖ crowded.

   Ⓗ dirty.

   Ⓙ sparkling.

   *Hint: The suffix "-ious" means* characterized by.

He had said some pretty bad things to the teacher when he saw her after school. Maybe he had just had enough of being called upon in class when he was unprepared. In retrospect, however, he was sorry he had lost his temper. He vowed to meet with his teacher the next morning to make things right.

3. In this paragraph, what does the word retrospect mean?

   _____respect_____ again___

   _____

   _____

   _____

   _____

   *Hint: "Retro-" is a prefix that means* backwards.

▶GO ON

Unit 2
Core Skills Test Prep, Grade 7

# OBJECTIVE 1: DETERMINING WORD MEANINGS

> ✓ Sometimes you can figure out the meaning of a new or difficult word by using the words around it as clues.

A woman in Australia and a woman in England were pen pals for a long time. Their <u>correspondence</u> lasted over 75 years.

1.  In this paragraph, the word <u>correspondence</u> means —

    Ⓐ letter writing.

    Ⓑ friends.

    Ⓒ phone calls.

    Ⓓ mailbox.

    *Hint: You get a clue as to what the word* <u>correspondence</u> *means in the first sentence.*

At the beach, there is a contest for building castles from the sand. Some of the castles are very <u>elaborate</u>. They have towers, windows, and even bridges.

2.  In this paragraph, the word <u>elaborate</u> means —

    Ⓕ sandy.

    Ⓖ short.

    Ⓗ plain.

    Ⓙ fancy.

    *Hint: You get a clue as to what the word* <u>elaborate</u> *means by reading the description of the castles in the last sentence.*

Animals that live in the desert are well protected. Their small bodies help them escape the heat that <u>scorches</u> the ground. Some animals stay in tunnels when the hot sun beats down.

3.  In this paragraph, the word <u>scorches</u> means —

    _____ burn _____

    _____

    _____

    _____

    _____

    _____

    *Hint: You get a clue as to what* <u>scorches</u> *means by the numerous references to heat.*

# OBJECTIVE 1: DETERMINING WORD MEANINGS

Specialized or technical words are words used in subjects such as science and social studies. You can use all the other information in the text to help figure out the meaning of these words.

In 1902, a man asked a woman to marry him. She said, "Yes." They decided to wait a few years before they got married. They finally got around to matrimony in 1969.

1. In this paragraph, the word matrimony means —

   Ⓐ talking.

   Ⓑ trying.

   Ⓒ marrying.

   Ⓓ dying.

   *Hint: You get a clue as to what the word matrimony means by reading the many references to marriage throughout.*

In 1980, someone threw a grape more than three hundred feet. A man caught the grape in his mouth. The site of this event was a football field in Louisiana.

2. In this paragraph, the word site means —

   Ⓕ toss.

   Ⓖ place.

   Ⓗ time.

   Ⓙ game.

   *Hint: Site is a technical word. You get a clue as to what it means in the sentence in which it appears.*

Pepper was once very rare. Armies seized it when they took over a city. In the fifth century, the Romans had to give three thousand pounds of it to enemies. Besides pepper, the winners also took gold, silver, and silk as part of their booty.

3. In this paragraph, the word booty means —

   _____ treasure _____

   _____

   _____

   _____

   _____

   _____

   _____

   *Hint: Booty is a technical word. You get a clue as to what it means from reading the entire paragraph.*

**9**

# OBJECTIVE 1: DETERMINING WORD MEANINGS

A word can have different meanings depending on when and how you use it. Readers can figure out the correct meaning of a word by reading the entire passage.

No one could call him dishonest. If he found a wallet with $100 in it, he would return it to its owner. He was a just man.

1. In this passage, the word just means —
   Ⓐ rich.
   Ⓑ phony.
   Ⓒ only.
   Ⓓ righteous.

   *Hint: Read the whole passage to determine what kind of man he was.*

Wanda came into the room looking for Rochelle. I told her that Rochelle had just left.

2. In this passage, the word just means —
   Ⓕ only.
   Ⓖ a very short time ago.
   Ⓗ never.
   Ⓙ a very long time ago.

   *Hint: You must read the whole selection to determine the meaning.*

As we walked through it, I saw how beautiful the estate of the foreign diplomat was. Each building within the compound was more beautiful than the last.

3. In this passage, the word compound means —
   Ⓐ combination of elements.
   Ⓑ enclosed space containing buildings.
   Ⓒ architectural drawing.
   Ⓓ painting.

   *Hint: Read both sentences to determine the meaning.*

The chemist invented a new compound. He hoped this mixture would give him the recognition he deserved.

4. In this passage, the word compound means —
   Ⓕ combination of elements.
   Ⓖ enclosed space.
   Ⓗ architectural drawing.
   Ⓙ painting.

   *Hint: You must read both sentences to determine the meaning.*

**STOP**

**10**

# OBJECTIVE 2: IDENTIFYING SUPPORTING IDEAS

Facts or details are important. By noticing and remembering them, you will know what the passage is about.

Many hundreds of years ago, a monk from India traveled to China. He began teaching people special movements to train the mind and body. His students learned to sit very still for a long time, breathing slowly. They learned shadowboxing and hand movements. All these movements came to be called *kung fu*.

When a Japanese army invaded a Chinese island, kung fu experts came to the rescue. They turned back the spears of the Japanese with their bare hands. The amazed Japanese called this weapon *kara* (empty) *te* (hand). Some Japanese then learned karate themselves, keeping it a secret for centuries. But after World War II, American soldiers discovered karate. The secret was no longer a secret. Teachers opened schools for people wanting to learn this ancient art. Today, karate schools are all over the world.

1. A monk came from India to —
   Ⓐ China.
   Ⓑ Japan.
   Ⓒ America.
   Ⓓ an island.
   *Hint: Look at the first sentence.*

2. Now karate schools are —
   Ⓕ for fighters.
   Ⓖ in Japan.
   Ⓗ for strong hands.
   Ⓙ all over the world.
   *Hint: Look at the last sentence in the second paragraph.*

3. How did Chinese kung fu experts turn back the Japanese?

   with there bare
   hands

   _____

   _____

   _____

   _____

   _____

   *Hint: Look at the second sentence in the second paragraph.*

GO ON

**11**

# OBJECTIVE 2: IDENTIFYING SUPPORTING IDEAS

> Sometimes it is helpful to arrange events in the order they happened. This may help you to understand a passage better.

The Mohawks once lived in Canada, but they grew weary of battling with the Algonquins there. So they moved south and settled on the banks of the Hudson River. Occasionally, however, some made short trips back to their old home. On one trip, enemies captured the Mohawk chief and his oldest son. The chief's wife and younger son grieved deeply. "I will find my father and brother and return with them," declared the boy. "Every night, Mother, build a fire on this cliff. The light will guide us home."

The woman built a fire every night. Years went by, and she continued to wait. Every night she sat by the fire in sorrow, and her tears tumbled down the cliff. Finally, one night, her younger son climbed the cliff, carrying the bones of his father and brother. He and his mother wept together. Then Manitou, the Great Spirit, sent lightning to carry them to his home in the sky. That same bolt of lightning transformed the woman's tears to crystal, and today her crystal tears still glisten on Diamond Rock.

1. Which of these happened first in the story?

   (A) The Mohawks moved south to the Hudson River.

   (B) A chief and his son traveled back to their old home.

   (C) Enemies captured the Mohawk chief and his son.

   (D) The chief's wife and younger son grieved.

   *Hint: Read the beginning to find what happened first.*

2. When did the younger son and his mother weep?

   (F) before the son went in search of his father and brother

   (G) on a trip down the Hudson River

   (H) after the son returned with the bones of his father and brother

   (J) when the son built a fire on the cliff

   *Hint: Read sentences 4 and 5 in the second paragraph.*

3. When did the younger son leave home?

   When the mohawk cheif was capturel

   _____

   _____

   _____

   _____

   _____

   *Hint: Read sentences 4 and 6 in the first paragraph.*

# OBJECTIVE 2: IDENTIFYING SUPPORTING IDEAS

Written directions tell the reader how to do something. To follow them means to do them in the same order in which they are given.

It seemed simple enough, so Peter did not know why his mother was making such a big deal out of it. The college coach had called and asked him to send him a copy of his football schedule and high school transcript. They were considering giving him an athletic scholarship.

Peter went to the guidance office and got a copy of the transcript and walked to the post office to mail it. When he got there, he realized he had left the football schedule at home, so he went home and got that. Back at the post office, he realized that he needed an envelope and also that he should make copies of each item so that he would have them to send to other colleges that might call. So he left the post office again and went to the stationery store to make copies and buy envelopes. Luckily, he met his friend Tom, so that he could borrow a dollar to make copies.

Carrying the growing number of items in hand, Peter went back to the post office and started to address the envelope. Where was it going? He knew the coach's name, but not his address. So he called his sister from the pay phone in the lobby and asked her to read the return address of the school from the envelope on the kitchen counter. Finally, he folded the transcript and schedule in thirds, put them in the envelope, put a stamp on it (after waiting in line to buy one), and put it in the out-of-town slot in the lobby. Big deal.

1. What was the first thing that Peter did?
   - (A) got a copy of his high school transcript
   - (B) got a copy of his football schedule
   - (C) had copies of his transcript made
   - (D) went to the guidance office and asked about what he needed

   *Hint: Read the start of the passage until you come to the answer.*

2. Before he spoke with Tom, Peter had realized all but one of the following —
   - (F) that he needed the football schedule.
   - (G) that he needed an envelope.
   - (H) that he needed to make copies.
   - (J) that he needed the coach's address.

   *Hint: Make a list of what Tom realized before he met his friend.*

3. What did Peter do after he made the copies?

   He went 7o the Post office

   *Hint: Read the part when Peter makes copies.*

STOP

# OBJECTIVE 2: IDENTIFYING SUPPORTING IDEAS

The setting of a passage lets you know when and where the passage is taking place.

It was a gray November day in 1963. A fishing boat rocked in the Atlantic Ocean off the southern coast of Iceland. Suddenly, a great black cloud burst from the water. Loud noises rumbled from the ocean, too. The ship's captain sent out a radio call. Something very unusual was happening!

During the next three hours, many scientists and reporters arrived at the scene. By now the cloud was 12,000 feet high. Huge explosions sent ash, dust, and hot rocks into the air. The watchers could see something just under the water's surface. A fiery island was growing in the Atlantic. It was caused by a volcano in the ocean.

1. The fiery island started growing in the year —
   - (A) 1993.
   - (B) 1936.
   - (C) 1963.
   - (D) 1863.

   *Hint: This asks about when the passage takes place.*

2. The fishing boat was off the coast of —
   - (F) Ireland.
   - (G) Greenland.
   - (H) Iceland.
   - (J) November.

   *Hint: This asks about where the passage takes place.*

3. During what season did the volcano erupt?

   _springs_

   _____

   _____

   _____

   _____

   _____

   *Hint: This asks about when the passage takes place.*

**STOP**

**14**

# OBJECTIVE 3: SUMMARIZING MAIN IDEAS

---

The main idea is the meaning of a piece of writing. Many times it is written in the passage.

---

Allied soldiers in World War II were trapped at Dunkirk, France, and they could not escape because the shallow water kept rescue ships from landing. But hundreds of people in England took rowboats, tugs, and barges across the English Channel. For eight days, this odd navy carried soldiers from the beaches to the large ships. More than 300,000 soldiers were taken to safety.

1. What is the main idea of this passage?

   Ⓐ Small ships are better than big ships.

   Ⓑ Many soldiers were saved.

   Ⓒ Soldiers were rescued from Dunkirk by the English.

   Ⓓ The big ships could not get into shallow water.

   *Hint: What does the whole passage talk about?*

Sharks have a number of "tools" that help them find food. They have a keen sense of hearing and can smell blood from almost 2,000 yards away. They also have a special system of channels in their skin that helps them feel the vibrations of a struggling swimmer. We know that in clear water, sharks can see their prey from about fifty feet away.

2. What is the main idea of this selection?

   Ⓕ Sharks hear well.

   Ⓖ Sharks have poor vision.

   Ⓗ Sharks sense food in a special way.

   Ⓙ Sharks like struggling swimmers.

   *Hint: What does the entire passage talk about?*

Every year, hungry deer do millions of dollars' worth of damage to young pine trees. But scientists in Washington have found a way to protect the trees using a substance called selenium. Selenium produces a bad smell when dissolved. A bit of this element is put in the ground near trees. Rain dissolves the selenium, and the tree absorbs it. The bad smell keeps the deer away until the tree is fully grown.

3. What is the main idea of this passage?

   A hungry deer doing millions of dollars.

   *Hint: What is most of the passage about?*

# OBJECTIVE 3: SUMMARIZING MAIN IDEAS

Often the main idea is not given in the text. Sometimes the reader needs to figure it out by putting the facts together.

Eleanor Roosevelt dedicated her life to children, the underprivileged, and the poor. She taught at a school that she set up for poor children and ran a factory for the jobless. Mrs. Roosevelt worked hard to help needy people during the Great Depression. Then after World War II, she worked as Chairman of the Human Rights Commission. She was a person who dedicated her life to helping others.

1. The main idea of the passage is —
   - Ⓐ She was a person who dedicated her life to helping others.
   - Ⓑ She taught at a school.
   - Ⓒ She ran a factory for the jobless.
   - Ⓓ She worked as a chairman of the Human Rights Commission.

   *Hint: What is the entire paragraph trying to suggest?*

Alfred Nobel invented dynamite to help builders. But it was used for war, which made him feel very guilty. He was a rich man, so he set up a $9 million fund. Today the fund is used to reward people who have improved human life. Nobel prizes are awarded in six fields including peace, medicine, and chemistry.

2. What is the main idea implied in the passage?
   - Ⓕ Nobel wanted to have a positive impact on society.
   - Ⓖ Nobel was afraid of failure.
   - Ⓗ Nobel wanted his invention used for more purposes.
   - Ⓙ Nobel's invention proved useless for building purposes.

   *Hint: Read the entire paragraph to determine the main idea suggested.*

Do you know the difference between bees and wasps? Bees and wasps both have wings, eyes, and six legs. A bee has lots of hair on its body. On the other hand, a wasp does not have any hair on its body. Some types of bees and wasps are very social, while others live alone. Honeybees live in colonies with many other bees and build a honeycomb out of wax. Wasps live in holes in the ground or in nests made from paper or mud. Wasps are meat eaters, while bees make their food from flowers. When a bee stings it dies, but wasps can sting again.

3. What is the main idea of this passage?

   _____

   _____

   _____

   _____

   _____

   _____

   _____

   *Hint: What is suggested, but not stated, in the passage?*

**GO ON**

# OBJECTIVE 3: SUMMARIZING MAIN IDEAS

A summary contains the main idea of a passage. A summary is brief, yet it covers the main points.

Aluminum once was a very expensive metal. It cost more than $500 a pound. But in 1886, two scientists discovered a way to make the metal more cheaply. Two years later, another scientist refined the process even more. Then the price of the metal was less than 30¢ a pound. Today aluminum is so cheap that it is often thrown away.

1. What is the best summary of this passage?

   Ⓐ Aluminum used to cost a lot of money.

   Ⓑ The price of aluminum has lowered over the years.

   Ⓒ Scientists have refined the process of making aluminum foil.

   Ⓓ Aluminum is a strong metal.

   *Hint: Look for the statement that sums up the passage.*

Product codes are the bars and numbers on a product label. The first numbers tell which company made the item. The last numbers identify the product and size. A laser reads the bars at the checkout. The computer finds the price for that product and prints the price on the cash register receipt. Store owners can change prices of items simply by changing the computer. The records stored in the computer also help stores to determine which items sell well.

2. What is this passage mostly about?

   Ⓕ Product codes were developed to ensure customer safety.

   Ⓖ A product code system is an efficient way of pricing goods.

   Ⓗ A machine can read numbers and bars.

   Ⓙ Numbers are assigned to companies.

   *Hint: Which statement best describes the passage as a whole?*

In 1815, Mount Tambora in Indonesia blew its top. The huge blast cut 4,000 feet off its peak, and it killed 12,000 people. The dust from the explosion spread around the world. It blocked the sunlight. Europe and America were very cold the following year. In June, ten inches of snow fell in New England. The year 1816 was called the year without any summer.

3. What is this passage mostly about?

(A) Many people died because of Mount Tambora.

(B) A volcanic explosion in 1815 had a major impact.

(C) People gave an unusual name to the year 1816.

(D) Ten inches of snow fell in New England in June.

*Hint: You need to read the entire passage to determine the best summary.*

Air plants, such as mosses and lichens, grow on buildings and stones and get their food and water from the air around them. Plants that grow on trees, such as mistletoe, get their food and water from the trees they live on. Sometimes, the trees die if the plants growing on them take away too much food or water.

4. What is this passage mostly about?

(F) Some kinds of plants grow on buildings.

(G) Mistletoe sometimes kills trees.

(H) Some plants don't have to live in soil to survive.

(J) Mosses and lichens get food and water in various ways.

*Hint: Pick the choice that best covers the main point of the passage.*

STOP

# OBJECTIVE 4: PERCEIVING RELATIONSHIPS AND RECOGNIZING OUTCOMES

Often when we read, we need to see cause-and-effect relationships. Knowing what happened and what made it happen will help us to better understand what we read.

Rodney bragged to his friends that he could find his way around anywhere. One day, though, Rodney was delivering pizza in a strange part of town. Though he searched for half an hour, he could not locate the address he needed. Finally, he had to stop to ask for directions. His face turned red, and he began to stutter as he asked how to find the place.

1. What happened when Rodney got embarrassed?
   A  He got overheated.
   B  He got lost.
   C  His face got red and he stuttered.
   D  He started bragging.

   *Hint: Getting embarrassed is the cause. What happened as a result of this?*

Over the years Jason and his dog, Flash, had shared many good times and great adventures. They played together, and sometimes they even slept together. But Flash got old, and his eyesight and hearing began to fade. He even started snapping at children, so Jason knew the time had come to put Flash to sleep. Although the idea of taking Flash to the vet made Jason very sad, he knew it was for the best.

2. What made Jason know the time had come to put Flash to sleep?
   F  Jason loved his dog Flash.
   G  Jason knew the vet needed business.
   H  Flash began to snap at children.
   J  Jason was very sad.

   *Hint: Knowing the time had come to put Flash to sleep is the effect. What made this happen?*

Angela did not like to go to the park any more. She used to spend her springtime afternoons there, enjoying the flowers and the fresh air. But now she saw more and more old people in the park, sitting alone on the benches. They seemed so sad and lonely that Angela wished she never had to grow old.

3. What caused Angela to dislike going to the park?
   A  She worried that she would become allergic to the flowers.
   B  She saw too many lonely old people.
   C  She was afraid that she might be robbed.
   D  The change of seasons made it less comfortable.

   *Hint: Not going to the park is the effect. Pick the choice that made this happen.*

The young man wouldn't listen to anyone. He was too sure of himself and felt he could handle any situation. Others had warned him not to camp alone in the freezing weather, but he did not listen to them. When he fell into icy water, he could not build a fire to warm himself. No one was there to help him.

4. What caused the young man to get into trouble?

   _____

   _____

   _____

   *Hint: Getting into trouble is the effect. What made this happen?*

**GO ON**

**19**

# OBJECTIVE 4: PERCEIVING RELATIONSHIPS AND RECOGNIZING OUTCOMES

Often, the reader can predict, or tell in advance, what is probably going to happen next. The reader must think about what would make sense if the story were to continue.

High school had not been an easy time for Diane. Her friends seemed to have so much more time for fun than she did. That just made today even more special. As she walked up the steps in her black cap and gown, she felt a real sense of pride. Glancing over at her parents, she saw her mother wipe a tear from her cheek.

1. What will probably happen next?
   (A) Diane will go to the library to study.
   (B) Diane will receive her diploma.
   (C) The family will go to dinner together.
   (D) Diane will give her mother a handkerchief.

   *Hint: Once you figure out what Diane is doing, you will know the answer.*

May's parents were having guests for dinner. Her mother asked May to help set the table. She noticed that May was trying to carry too many dishes at one time. May loaded down a tray with ten crystal glasses and had trouble lifting the heavy tray. Her mother had warned her, but May paid no attention.

2. What will May probably do next?
   (F) drop the tray
   (G) set the table
   (H) serve the guests
   (J) stop listening to her mother

   *Hint: Think about what the passage seems to be leading toward.*

It was Jonathan's first day at his new school. Before school, groups of students gathered in front of the building. It seemed as if everyone but Jonathan was with a group of friends. They were all talking and laughing together. He walked over to a bench and sat down to read. Then he noticed someone coming toward him. It was Paul, a boy he had met last summer at the local pool.

3. What will Jonathan probably do next?
   (A) get up and leave
   (B) go over to the group of students
   (C) say hello to Paul as he comes closer
   (D) ask Paul if he wants to go to the pool with him again

   *Hint: Based on the other sentences, what seems most likely to happen next?*

To Sheila, the alarm clock seemed to go off especially early that morning. She forced herself out of bed and put on her running clothes. Once she was outside, the cold air helped her wake up. It was just a few days before the race, and she wanted to be in top condition.

4. What will Sheila probably do next?

   _____

   _____

   _____

   *Hint: You need to look at all the facts in the story. What is most likely to happen next?*

# OBJECTIVE 5: MAKING INFERENCES AND GENERALIZATIONS

Often texts come with graphs or diagrams. They help the reader better understand the passage.

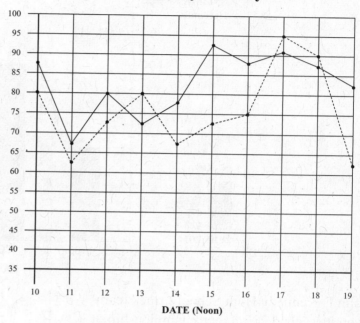

**Temperature and Humidity for Ten Days in May**

**KEY**

———— Temperature in Degrees

---------- Humidity in Percent

The weather in Florida varies somewhat, but it always seems that there is a lot of humidity in May. Both the temperature and humidity vary considerably. Low humidity with warm temperatures is the perfect type of weather for the beach. The discomfort and perspiration index seem to rise as the humidity rises.

1. On which day did both the humidity and temperature drop about twenty percent?

   (A) May 11

   (B) May 13

   (C) May 15

   (D) May 16

   *Hint: Check the "Temperature" and "Humidity" lines for each of the dates in the choices.*

2. According to the graph, which would be the worst beach day? Why?

   _____

   _____

   _____

   _____

   _____

   _____

   _____

   *Hint: First decide what would make up the worst beach day, according to the author.*

**GO ON**

**21**

### John F. Kennedy High School's
### Best Race Times

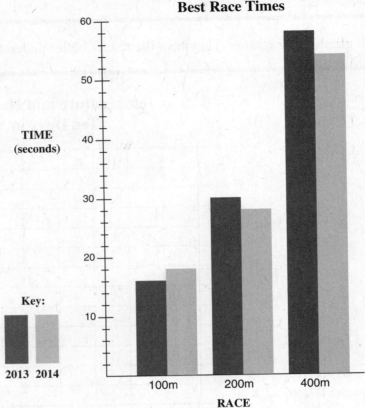

Key:
2013   2014

John F. Kennedy High School's track team has won its second 200m race championship. It finished both the 100m and 400m in second place. Although Kennedy has a good team, Wedgewood High School had an outstanding year. They edged Kennedy in both the 100m and 400m but were not able to beat them in the 200m.

3. In the 2014 championship 200m race, the time it took Wedgewood High to run the race could have been —

   Ⓕ  32 seconds.

   Ⓖ  28 seconds.

   Ⓗ  26 seconds.

   Ⓙ  24 seconds.

   *Hint: Look at the bars on the graph that show Kennedy High's 200m time.*

4. In which race did the Kennedy High team's performance get worse from 2013 to 2014?

   _____

   _____

   _____

   _____

   _____

   _____

   _____

   _____

   *Hint: Read both the graph and the key that accompanies it.*

Core Skills Test Prep, Grade 7

GO ON ▶

# OBJECTIVE 5: MAKING INFERENCES AND GENERALIZATIONS

> When a reader makes an inference, it means that the information in the passage has told the reader something indirectly.

El Santo was a famous fellow in Mexico. He was successful as a wrestler, but he was also a top movie star. In his movies, he played a masked wrestler who helped catch criminals and monsters. His best film was *The Mummies of Guanajuato*. El Santo died in 1984.

1.  What conclusion can you draw after reading this passage?

    Ⓐ  The wrestler performed good deeds.

    Ⓑ  El Santo hated wrestling.

    Ⓒ  The Mexican people like wrestling.

    Ⓓ  El Santo died at the hands of a criminal.

    *Hint: First eliminate the choices that you think cannot be right.*

When people began to grow crops, they needed to know when to plant their seeds. They noticed that the best time to plant came at the same time each year. The early Egyptians counted the number of full moons between planting times. The times between moons were called months of the year. The Egyptians then noticed a bright star in the sky at planting time. They counted 365 days between the appearances of this star. Then they divided these days by 12 months to invent the first year.

2.  What can you conclude after reading this?

    Ⓕ  Egyptians invented the first calendar.

    Ⓖ  The Egyptians invented time.

    Ⓗ  The Egyptians were astronomers.

    Ⓙ  The Egyptians counted one day every time the star appeared.

    *Hint: Although never stated, the selection is describing the invention of something.*

The ancient Greeks made up stories to explain their world. They thought that many gods and goddesses controlled the universe. The greatest Greek god was Zeus, who controlled the weather. When a storm raged with thunder and lightning, Zeus was at work. The Greeks believed that the natural world was alive and that it should be treated with respect.

3.  What is inferred by this passage?

    Ⓐ  The Greeks did not understand science.

    Ⓑ  The Greeks thought Zeus controlled the universe.

    Ⓒ  The ancient Greeks weren't smart.

    Ⓓ  The Greeks thought Zeus was the least powerful god.

    *Hint: Look for the choice that is not written in the passage, but implied.*

Charlene awoke with a shriek. Her pajamas were soaked with sweat, and she could feel herself trembling. The night was dark and still, and the furniture in her room loomed like shadowy monsters. Charlene closed her eyes and tried to fall asleep again. But the night was too quiet, and her eyes popped open. Suddenly, Charlene heard a scratching noise at her window. She buried her head under her pillow, wishing the night was over.

4.  What can you infer after reading this?

    _____

    _____

    _____

    *Hint: Think about this happening to you.*

▶ GO ON

**23**

# OBJECTIVE 5: MAKING INFERENCES AND GENERALIZATIONS

Sometimes a reader needs to generalize. This means to come up with a general statement about something in the text.

The special material in our body that makes us who we are is called DNA. Except for identical twins, everybody has different DNA. Since DNA is everywhere in the body, scientists believe that DNA patterns are better than fingerprints for identifying people.

1. From this passage you can make the generalization that —
   (A) DNA may become a commonly used way of identifying people.
   (B) identical twins have the same fingerprints.
   (C) fingerprints are the best way for the police to fight crime.
   (D) DNA patterns for identical twins are similar.

   *Hint: Read the whole paragraph. Generalize what might happen in the future.*

A comet is like a dirty ball of snow. It is made of frozen gases, frozen water, and dust. As a comet approaches the sun, the icy center gets hot and evaporates. The gases made by the evaporation form the tail of the comet. The dust left behind in the process forms meteor showers.

2. From this paragraph you can guess that —
   (F) comets are made of snow.
   (G) throwing a ball of snow can turn it into a comet.
   (H) without the sun, a comet would look different to us.
   (J) meteor showers are visible with a telescope.

   *Hint: Which choice is the best "guess"?*

Nations fight wars for many reasons. In the 1880s, a war between the United States and Great Britain almost started because of a pig. The trouble took place on an island off the coast of Washington state. An American shot a pig owned by a British man. Tempers flared, and troops were sent to the island. The dispute, known as the Pig War, was soon settled without any fighting.

3. The passage suggests that —
   (A) many soldiers were injured in the war.
   (B) the war was fought in Europe.
   (C) the pig was cooked when the war ended.
   (D) in the 1880s, the Americans and British did not get along well.

   *Hint: Which choice is a general statement rather than a specific one?*

Mongooses are small Asian mammals that kill poisonous snakes and, sometimes, rats. In the 1890s, sugar planters in Hawaii imported mongooses to control the rats there. But the planters made a big mistake. They learned too late that mongooses roam by day, while rats roam by night. Now mongooses are a problem in Hawaii.

4. How did the sugar planters make their problems worse?

   _____

   _____

   _____

   _____

   *Hint: What is the general idea of this passage?*

# OBJECTIVE 5: MAKING INFERENCES AND GENERALIZATIONS

A good reader will evaluate what he or she reads and make his or her own judgment about the text. Often things are implied in a text, rather than stated directly.

Tom Evans was on a field trip in Big Bend National Park in Texas. He and his college classmates had come from Chicago to hunt for fossils. As he was searching, Evans spotted something sticking out of a dirt mound. It turned out to be a major discovery. Evans had found the complete skull of a dinosaur. The four-foot-long skull came from a chasmosaurus, which resembled a rhinoceros. The skull had been buried for about eighty million years.

1. What does this passage tell you about Tom Evans?
   Ⓐ He was a straight-A student.
   Ⓑ He flew from Chicago to Big Bend National Park.
   Ⓒ He was an observant person.
   Ⓓ He enjoyed gardening.

   *Hint: Review the facts. Think about what they say about Tom.*

Longfellow wrote a poem that made Paul Revere famous for his ride to Concord to warn people that the British were coming. Actually, Revere never made it to Concord, nor was he alone. Two other riders, William Dawes and Dr. Samuel Prescott, went with him. It was Dr. Prescott who warned Concord about the British.

2. From the paragraph, you can tell that —
   Ⓕ the people of Concord weren't warned.
   Ⓖ Paul Revere had a friend named William Dawes.
   Ⓗ Longfellow was famous for his poetry.
   Ⓙ because of a well-known poem, people are misinformed about historical facts.

   *Hint: You need to read the entire paragraph and evaluate the information before making a choice.*

The Agriculture Department inspects packages from foreign countries. It makes sure that plant diseases aren't brought into the country. Dogs are trained to sniff for food. When the dogs smell food, they sit down by the passenger carrying it.

3. From the passage, you can tell that —
   Ⓐ the Agriculture Department provides us with an important safeguard.
   Ⓑ dogs bring a lot of disease into North America.
   Ⓒ it is not good to alert officials to food packages.
   Ⓓ food should be grown in North America and not imported.

   *Hint: None of the choices are stated in the passage, but one of them is a conclusion that the reader can determine after reading the text.*

When men sip drinks from cups, they usually look into them. Women usually look above the rim. Men often examine their nails with their palms facing upward and their fingers curled. But women extend their fingers with their palms facing downward to view their nails.

4. What judgment can you make about men and women after reading this paragraph?

   _____

   _____

   _____

   _____

   *Hint: Read the entire paragraph. Think about the point that is being made.*

**25**

# OBJECTIVE 5: MAKING INFERENCES AND GENERALIZATIONS

The setting is the when and where of a story. The characters are the people or people-like figures in the story. The plot is the sequence of events that makes up the core of the story.

Ilse Bing was a photographer in the 1930s. She was one of the first photographers to use a camera to make works of art. Cameras had been around since the late 1800s. However, most photographers used them to take pictures of news events or famous people. Bing took photos of people who were dressed beautifully or oddly.

At about the same time, Laura Gilpin was working in the American Southwest. She took pictures as she hiked through the desert. One of Gilpin's most famous pictures is called "Shiprock, New Mexico." It shows a gigantic rock standing alone in a valley. Gilpin made many of her prints on a special soft paper. The special paper made her prints look cloudy and gray, like old paintings.

1. Ilse Bing was a photographer in the —
   (A) nineteenth century.
   (B) twentieth century.
   (C) eighteenth century.
   (D) twenty-first century.

   *Hint: Read the first sentence.*

2. Laura Gilpin was working in —
   (F) the east.          (H) the southwest.
   (G) the midwest.       (J) the west.

   *Hint: Read the paragraph about Gilpin.*

3. How were their photographs different?

   _____

   _____

   *Hint: Read about both women's photos.*

Louise and her mother were driving home one evening. They had been visiting Louise's aunt. Louise soon noticed that her mother was slowing down. It was getting impossible to see the road. For the next hour, their car crept slowly along the road. Headlights would suddenly appear in front of them, and they would move as far to the right of the road as they could. Both women were praying that they would get home safely.

4. What is the setting of this passage?
   (A) It was a bright night.
   (B) It was dark and foggy.
   (C) It was a poorly paved road.
   (D) There were large potholes in the road.

   *Hint: Picture the scene in your mind. Which choice seems most like that picture?*

5. What conclusion can you draw about the characters' mood in this passage?

   _____

   _____

   _____

   _____

   _____

   _____

   *Hint: Think about how you might feel in the same situation.*

STOP

Name _____ Date _____

# OBJECTIVE 6: RECOGNIZING POINTS OF VIEW, FACTS, AND OPINIONS

> The author's point of view is what he or she thinks or feels about what he or she is writing. Opinions express points of view.

The National Park System costs $1.2 billion to operate. Of that amount, $900,000 is spent on costs associated with visitors. The system has 368 locations, including major parks, such as the Grand Canyon, and small, specialized parks that feature one thing. We need to reexamine the type and quality of parks paid for by federal dollars. An independent commission could review the parks and determine whether or not they all should be kept open and what level of fees should be charged to park users. Currently, the people who use parks pay less than ten percent of the costs of operating them.

1. What is the author suggesting?
   - Ⓐ A commission should start closing the smaller parks.
   - Ⓑ The government should pay a larger portion of the costs of running the national parks.
   - Ⓒ There is a need to reexamine the current parks to be sure we want to keep them and see if we need them all.
   - Ⓓ The National Park System will be fine if we just eliminate some of the smaller specialized parks.

   *Hint: In this passage, the author's point of view is clearly stated in sentences 4 and 5.*

2. The author would agree with which of the following?
   - Ⓕ The National Park System should continue as it is.
   - Ⓖ Government systems waste time and money.
   - Ⓗ It is good to reevaluate things as time goes on.
   - Ⓙ The park system should be shut down.

   *Hint: Think about the author's point of view regarding the National Park System and figure out what he or she would most likely think about the choices given.*

3. Should some national parks be closed because they are too expensive to run? Explain your answer.

   _____
   _____
   _____
   _____
   _____
   _____
   _____

   *Hint: Use the information in the paragraph to form your opinion.*

▶GO ON▶

**27**

© Houghton Mifflin Harcourt Publishing Company

Unit 2
Core Skills Test Prep, Grade 7

People are concerned that irradiated food will lead to an increase in cancer. But what about the benefits of reduced toxins, food decontamination, and a longer shelf life? Have x-rays caused people to become radioactive? Irradiation eliminates poisonous toxins and microorganisms. Scientists have found more of a chemical reaction in frozen and canned food than in food that has been irradiated. Sixty-seven percent of consumers would be willing to pay more for chicken that has significantly fewer toxins, according to a recent survey.

4. With which statement would this author most likely agree?

    Ⓐ  Frozen foods are safer than irradiated foods.

    Ⓑ  X-rays cause people to become radioactive.

    Ⓒ  People are foolish to worry about cancer.

    Ⓓ  Irradiation reduces the risks of contamination.

*Hint: The answer is stated in the passage.*

5. What is the author's purpose in writing this selection?

    Ⓕ  to convince people that x-rays are unsafe

    Ⓖ  to convince people that x-rays are safe

    Ⓗ  to convince supermarkets to raise their prices

    Ⓙ  to convince people that irradiated food is safe

*Hint: Read the last sentence.*

6. List the benefits of irradiation that the author mentions in this paragraph.

_____

_____

_____

_____

_____

_____

_____

*Hint: Read the entire paragraph.*

GO ON

**28**

# OBJECTIVE 6: RECOGNIZING POINTS OF VIEW, FACTS, AND OPINIONS

When an author wants to convince the reader of something, he or she uses language that backs up his or her point of view. Often the language is very descriptive and emotional.

The money spent on political campaigns is paltry when compared to expenditures for commercial advertising. If we limited campaign spending, the incumbents would have an unfair advantage. Limiting campaign spending is like limiting free speech, which is embodied in the First Amendment of the Constitution. Maybe we should reform political campaigns, but not limit spending on them. What we really need to ensure is that all candidates who wish to can afford to campaign effectively.

1. The author is saying that —
   (A) campaigns cost too much.
   (B) campaign spending should not be limited.
   (C) there should be an amendment to the Constitution.
   (D) we should limit campaign spending.

   *Hint: Read the entire paragraph.*

2. When the author writes, "Limiting campaign spending is like limiting free speech," he is saying that —
   (F) we should limit free speech.
   (G) political campaigns should be free.
   (H) since free speech is limited, we should limit campaign spending.
   (J) limiting campaign spending is unconstitutional.

   *Hint: Read the entire sentence.*

National service can teach the values of hard work, self-sacrifice, and learning to live with different people. It can put our youth back to work. It can teach them job skills and instill the values of discipline, responsibility, and civic obligation. It can also provide long-term investment in the education and skills of our citizens. National service can also bring us together as a nation. We need to move back to a central core of beliefs.

3. What is the author promoting?
   (A) making long-term investments
   (B) writing a central core of beliefs
   (C) living with different people
   (D) starting a national service program

   *Hint: Read the entire paragraph.*

4. When the author writes, "It can also provide long-term investment in the education and skills of our citizens," she is trying to convince the reader that —
   (F) the benefits of national service can last a lifetime.
   (G) education is important to the citizens of this country.
   (H) national service is a long-term program.
   (J) education is more important than national service.

   *Hint: Reread the sentence in context.*

**GO ON**

29

# OBJECTIVE 6: RECOGNIZING POINTS OF VIEW, FACTS, AND OPINIONS

It is important to recognize the difference between fact and opinion. A fact is real and true. An opinion states a point of view. Words that describe are used to offer opinions.

Basketball is the only major sport that is a totally American game. Jim Naismith started it all. During the 1880s, Naismith taught athletics at a college in Massachusetts.

In the fall, Naismith's students spent long, exciting hours on the football field. But when winter came, the students moved indoors and did exercises. Most students soon grew bored. They kept asking for an indoor game that was as exciting as football.

Naismith began to think about a new kind of ball game that could be played safely in a small gym. He decided that players shouldn't use bats or run while holding the ball. Players would use only their hands to pass or throw the ball to other players. Naismith still had one big question. How would players score points? He went to the college store room and pulled out two peach baskets!

There was a balcony all around the gym. It was exactly ten feet above the floor. Naismith hung one peach basket on the balcony at each end of the gym. Then he divided the class into two teams of nine players each. The first basketball game began when he threw a soccer ball up between the team captains.

The players dashed up and down the gym, yelling with excitement as they tried to throw the ball into the peach baskets. The game stopped for a while when a player sank the ball. Someone climbed a ladder to get it out. After all, there is no hole in the bottom of a peach basket; but that was the only pause in the first basketball game. The final score was 1-0.

As basketball became popular at other colleges, teams made up their own rules. However, a set of rules was developed within a few years. A special ball and an open hoop took the place of the soccer ball and peach baskets. The game of basketball had begun.

1.  Which of the following is a fact about Jim Naismith?
    (A)  He was a good teacher.
    (B)  He taught athletics.
    (C)  He preferred indoor sports to outdoor sports.
    (D)  Basketball players are overpaid because of him.

    *Hint: A fact is real and true. What is actually said in the story?*

2.  Which of the following is a fact?
    (F)  Basketball is as exciting as football.
    (G)  College basketball is more exciting than high school basketball.
    (H)  Basketball would be a better game if the baskets were lowered.
    (J)  The game of basketball has a set of rules.

    *Hint: Facts have to be true all the time. What is said in the story?*

3.  Which of the following is *not* a fact from the story?
    (A)  The balcony was ten feet above the gym floor.
    (B)  Each team had nine players.
    (C)  Basketball is the only major sport that is totally American.
    (D)  Naismith taught athletics at a college in the 1980s.

    *Hint: Three of the statements can be found in the story. One is not true.*

## Ending World Hunger

In some parts of the world, food shortages cause many people to starve. No one should have to be hungry. Somehow people must find a way to increase the world's food crop.

To do this, governments should grant more money to scientists who are studying little-known, edible plants. There are currently about 20,000 kinds of edible plants. Only about 100 of them are grown as food crops. People should take advantage of natural foods. It is unfair to allow people to starve while plants are available for them to eat. A sensible solution to world hunger would be to direct government funds toward scientists. Spending money to end hunger in this way should be a goal for all governments.

4. Which of the following is a fact from the selection?

　Ⓕ　governments should grant money to scientists

　Ⓖ　there are about 20,000 kinds of edible plants

　Ⓗ　people should take advantage of natural foods

　Ⓙ　it is unfair to allow people to starve

*Hint: Read the second paragraph.*

5. The author's purpose in writing this selection is to —

　Ⓐ　persuade people to eat more plants.

　Ⓑ　describe the work of scientists.

　Ⓒ　explain the causes of world hunger.

　Ⓓ　propose a possible solution to food shortages.

*Hint: Read the last paragraph.*

6. What is the author's solution to world hunger?

_____

_____

_____

_____

_____

_____

_____

*Hint: Read the entire passage.*

**STOP**

**31**

# Unit 3: Reading Comprehension

## READING SELECTIONS

Directions: Read each selection carefully. Then read each question. Darken the circle for the correct answer, or write the answer in the space provided.

| Try This | More than one answer choice may seem correct. Choose the answer that goes best with the selection. |
|---|---|

**Sample A    Answering an Ad**

Josh had always wanted a pen pal. Therefore, he was excited to see the ad in his magazine guaranteeing to match people as pen pals. He followed the directions in the ad, and sent $5.00 and a brief letter describing himself to the address in the ad.

What did Josh hope to receive by following the directions in the ad?

Ⓐ  a pen

Ⓑ  $5.00

Ⓒ  a pen pal

Ⓓ  a magazine

| Think It Through | The correct answer is C. Josh wanted a pen pal, and the second sentence states that the ad guaranteed to match pen pals. |
|---|---|

**STOP**

## Adopting a Junior High School

Several schools in the southeastern part of our country were damaged or destroyed by a hurricane. These schools need help rebuilding in order to open by the first of October. The schools have asked for donations of school supplies.

Our school has adopted Jackson Junior High School in southern Florida. We will hold a school-supply drive to help the students of this school. The kinds of supplies needed include gym bags, locks for lockers, art boxes, scissors, pens and pencils, folders, and rulers. The school also needs books to help rebuild their school library.

The drive will begin on Monday, September 7, and end Friday, September 25. Please bring your donations to the school gym before or after school. Students who wish to pack items and label boxes should contact the principal. I would like to take this opportunity to thank all donators and volunteers in advance for your support.

1. Why was a school-supply drive being held for Jackson Junior High School?

Ⓐ  The school had burned down.

Ⓑ  The school had hurricane damage.

Ⓒ  The students were very poor.

Ⓓ  Supplies were ruined by a flood.

2. Besides making donations, what else does the school want students to do?

_____

_____

_____

_____

_____

# The 10K Mind Change

"A race? On foot? You're kidding," Nick said to his best friend, Emilio. "We're fleet of mind, not fleet of foot," he added, referring to the boys' skills as computer programmers. "Ten kilometers—that's more than six miles!"

"It's a piece of cake," Emilio told his friend. "It'll benefit our minds as well as our bodies," he said. "Come on, amigo—are we men or mice? Squeak up!"

Nick reluctantly agreed to enter his city's annual Heart to Heart 10K race but only if they could walk it, not run it. Forced to accept this compromise, Emilio mapped out a training schedule for the six weeks prior to the race. The boys met before school each morning. They stretched their muscles for a few minutes and then walked around the school track several times, adding a lap every few days and increasing their pace. Nick complained loudly and frequently about having to wake up early, about the stretching, about the "endless laps" around the track. Emilio was starting to lose patience with his unhappy friend. "I'm trying, I'm trying," Nick would protest.

"Yes, you are," Emilio would answer. "Very trying." The only thing that kept Emilio from giving up on his friend was that he noticed Nick had lost a few excess pounds and that he was walking—or trudging— slightly faster around the track each week.

On the day of the race, the boys positioned themselves near the starting line. "I can't believe you talked me into this," Nick moaned to his friend. At the sound of the starting gun, the pack moved forward in one huge wave. After the first fifty yards or so, the runners began to sort themselves out. Emilio and Nick let the remaining runners pass and began to find their rhythm.

As the boys settled into their pace, Emilio noticed that his friend's mood seemed to be improving. The spectators who lined the course clapped and shouted encouraging words to the participants. Emilio thought he saw a smile creep across Nick's face and noticed that his friend's gait quickened at the applause.

At last, the finish line came into sight. As the boys strode across it, Nick looked over at Emilio. "Well, I'm glad that's over," he said. "Now I can go back to a life of leisure."

The following Monday, Emilio arrived at school early to complete a science project, and as he approached the front door, something in the distance caught his eye. It was a lone figure, walking briskly around the school track, arms pumping energetically at his sides. Emilio smiled and entered the building.

**3.** Based on the context of paragraph 4, when Emilio says, "Very trying," what does *trying* mean?

   Ⓕ attempting

   Ⓖ annoying

   Ⓗ hardworking

   Ⓙ amusing

**4.** Which statement *best* summarizes the theme of the selection?

   Ⓐ Practice makes perfect.

   Ⓑ Experience can change a person's mind.

   Ⓒ Friendship is based on trust and respect.

   Ⓓ Winning is everything.

**5.** Explain how this story supports the idea that encouragement is powerful.

_____

_____

_____

_____

**6.** Why does Emilio smile at the end of the passage?

   Ⓕ He saw Nick walking.

   Ⓖ He gets to work on his science project.

   Ⓗ He got to school early.

   Ⓙ He is glad it is Monday.

**7.** What does Emilio mean when he says "It's a piece of cake"?

   Ⓐ It will be hard.

   Ⓑ We can eat cake after the race.

   Ⓒ It will be good for us.

   Ⓓ It will be easy.

**8.** In paragraph 6, what does *spectators* mean?

   Ⓕ people running the race

   Ⓖ people watching the race

   Ⓗ people walking the race

   Ⓙ people who have finished the race

**9.** When did the boys meet to train?

   Ⓐ after school

   Ⓑ during lunch

   Ⓒ before school

   Ⓓ on the weekends

**10.** How does Emilio encourage Nick to start training for the 10K?

_____

_____

_____

_____

_____

▶**GO ON**

**34**

# Notice for Eighth-Grade Students and Their Parents!

As you may know, all eighth-grade students are invited to participate in an outdoor education program. This program will once again be held at Fullersburg Outdoor Education Center, which is approximately 90 miles from our school.

Students will leave school the morning of the first day, travel by school bus to Fullersburg, sleep over three nights, and return the evening of the fourth day. All meals will be provided by the center. The school PTA has agreed to pay for the cost of room and board for each student. The school district will pay for the remaining costs, including the program and the bus transportation.

Participation in this program is open to all students who are able and willing to behave appropriately on an outing in which cooperation, respect for others, and following directions is expected. School behavior will be used to help determine the participants. Students who do not participate in the outdoor education program will attend classes at school.

All eighth-grade teachers and the principal will also attend the program as chaperons. The staff at Fullersburg will provide the instructional program.

Reservations for the trip must be made by completing the attached reservation form and returning it to the school by March 15.

# The Fullersburg Outdoor Education Center

Fullersburg Outdoor Education Center contains several hundred acres of wooded land along the Salt River. There are a variety of trees, a swamp area, and a dry creek bed. During the Great Depression the Civilian Conservation Corps planted trees and built shelters throughout the center.

The heated lodge at the center was completed in 1981. The lodge consists of a large classroom, a kitchen, a glassed-in dining area with a breathtaking view of the woods and river, a nature museum, two bunk rooms with bathrooms, and private sleeping quarters for chaperons.

The daily schedule for students at Fullersburg includes breakfast and clean-up, an outdoor activity with an instructional follow-up, lunch and clean-up, an outdoor activity with an instructional follow-up, supper and clean-up. After supper there are recreational activities. Before bedtime there are treats, an evening program, and then showers.

Some of the outdoor activities that students can choose include archery, horseback riding, hiking, orienteering, animal tracking, bird watching, fishing, and canoeing. If there is enough snow on the ground, students may choose cross-country skiing, sledding, or snowshoeing as an activity. If the river is frozen, students may play broom hockey or ice skate.

11. According to the flyer, the outdoor education program —

F  has never been held at Fullersburg before.

G  is usually held at the school.

H  has been held at Fullersburg in the past.

J  is held at different places each year.

12. According to the flyer, who is invited to participate in the outdoor education program?

A  all seventh- and eighth-grade students

B  eighth-grade students who are on the honor roll

C  eighth-grade students and their parents

D  all eighth-grade students who can behave properly

13. Costs for the outdoor education program will be paid for by —

F  the PTA and the school district.

G  the students.

H  the parents.

J  the teachers and community businesses.

14. Where would this notice most likely be found?

_____

_____

_____

15. According to the flyer, which of these statements is true?

A  Fullersburg is located several hundred miles from the school.

B  The students will need to provide their own transportation to the center.

C  Students who do not participate in the outdoor program will attend classes taught by the principal at the school.

D  The staff at Fullersburg will provide the instructional program.

16. Which of these statements is an *opinion* in the flyer?

F  The outdoor education center is located along the Salt River.

G  The heated lodge at the center was completed in 1981.

H  Students are expected to clean up after themselves.

J  The dining area has a breathtaking view of the woods and river.

17. According to the selection, the students can play broom hockey —

A  in the bunk rooms.

B  in the glassed-in dining room.

C  on the river if it is frozen.

D  in the large classroom.

18. What might be the author's purpose in writing this flyer?

_____

_____

_____

_____

**GO ON**

# The Sport of In-line Skating

Most people are familiar with roller-skating. In-line skating, however, is one of the fastest-growing sports in the world. In 1984 there were 20,000 in-line skaters. By 1992 there were more than three million in-line skaters.

In-line skates have a single row of polyurethane rollers attached to the bottom of a padded boot. The number of rollers on a skate can vary from three to five. At the rear of the skate is a heel stop.

I bought my first pair of in-line skates with money that I had saved from birthdays and from baby-sitting jobs. I bought a pair of four-wheeled skates for $65.00. I also decided to buy the safety equipment—gloves, helmet, kneepads, elbow pads, wrist guards—recommended by friends who are in-line skaters. I left the store broke, but *exhilarated.*

As soon as I got home I wanted to start skating. A friend who is a member of the International In-line Skating Association suggested that I learn to stop before I started to skate. She suggested that I practice on a safe grassy area. So I walked to a nearby park. I spent about an hour practicing to stop. When I felt comfortable stopping, I found an empty tennis court and I practiced skating strokes. I fell several times. Each time I fell, I was grateful that I was wearing the safety equipment. I'll never forget that day. My body was in pain, but my spirit was lifted by the thrill of gliding across cement.

It has been three years since I bought my first in-line skates. My friends and I belong to an in-line skating club. Our local YMCA allows us to use their rink, and the health club allows in-line skating an hour every day in the gym. I believe that my skills at in-line skating are good enough for me to become a professional skater.

**19.** In this selection, the word *exhilarated* means —

(F) exhausted.

(G) excited.

(H) excluded.

(J) expanded.

**20.** The selection implies that roller-skating is —

(A) as popular as in-line skating.

(B) more difficult than in-line skating.

(C) a sport of the past.

(D) not as safe as in-line skating.

**21.** What is at the rear of an in-line skate?

(F) a heel stop

(G) a polyurethane roller

(H) a safety guard

(J) a distance meter

**22.** Which of these is an *opinion* in the selection?

(A) In-line skating is one of the fastest-growing sports in the world.

(B) My skills at in-line skating are good enough for me to become a professional skater.

(C) In-line skates can have three, four, or five wheels.

(D) Safety equipment for in-line skating includes gloves, a helmet, kneepads, elbow pads, and wrist guards.

**23.** What should you do if you were asked to skim this selection?

(F) carefully reread the selection

(G) recall the main idea of the selection

(H) quickly look through the selection

(J) review your notes about the selection

**24.** The web shows some important ideas in the selection. Fill in the empty boxes with the missing information.

```
                    ┌─────────────────┐
                    │ In-line Skating │
                    └─────────────────┘
              ┌──────────┴──────────┐
      ┌───────────────────┐  ┌──────────────────┐
      │ Places to Practice│  │ Safety Equipment │
      └───────────────────┘  └──────────────────┘
       ┌────┬────┐            ┌──────┬──────┐
    ┌─────┐ ┌──────┐      ┌──────┐      ┌─────────┐
    │park │ │YMCA  │      │gloves│      │knee and │
    └─────┘ │rink  │      └──────┘      │elbow    │
            └──────┘        ┌────────┐  │pads     │
          ┌──────┐ ┌──────┐ │helmet  │  └─────────┘
          │gym   │ │      │ └────────┘
          └──────┘ └──────┘
```

**25.** Describe the author's first day on in-line skates.

_____

_____

_____

_____

_____

_____

_____

**GO ON**

### Schedule for Jefferson County Fair

| FRI. | 11:00–12:00 | 1:00 | 2:00 | 3:00 |
|------|-------------|------|------|------|
| | Judging of 4-H craft projects | Footraces - - - - - - - - - - - - - - - - - - - - - - - - - - → | | |
| | | Toddlers | 4-5 year olds | 6-8 year olds |
| SAT. | Pet parade | Footraces - - - - - - - - - - - - - - - - - - - - - - - - - - → | | |
| | Judging of 4-H farming projects | 9-10 year-olds | 11-12 year olds | 13-14 year olds |
| | | | Teddy bear picnic | |
| SUN. | Baby contest | Crowning of 4-H king and queen | Marching band contest | |
| | Judging of 4-H livestock projects | | | |

**26.** When is the marching band contest scheduled to take place?

(A) Sunday at 11:00

(B) Saturday at 2:00

(C) Sunday at 2:00

(D) Saturday at 11:00

**27.** How many events are scheduled for Sunday?

(F) 2

(G) 3

(H) 4

(J) 5

**28.** For a 4-H project, Kyle raised a pig named Rufus and entered it in the fair. When would Kyle learn if Rufus won a prize?

_____

_____

_____

_____

**29.** What event will be missed by the 11-12 year olds who participate in the footraces?

(A) Pet parade

(B) Crowning of king and queen

(C) Teddy bear picnic

(D) Baby contest

**30.** If 11-year-old Carole and 12-year-old Rachel entered the footraces, when would their race take place?

(F) Friday at 1:30

(G) Friday at 3:00

(H) Saturday at 1:30

(J) Saturday at 2:00

**31.** Where would you most likely find this schedule?

_____

_____

_____

_____

STOP

**39**

# Test

**Sample A**   Going Camping

Jen is very excited about going camping with her cousins Bill and Mindy. The cousins are good friends. The campers plan to travel to the Grand Canyon where they will stay for two weeks.

On their trip the three cousins most likely will —

(A) be very bored.

(B) fight and argue continually.

(C) have an enjoyable time.

(D) ignore one another.

**For questions 1–35 carefully read each selection and the questions that follow. Then darken the circle for the correct answer, or write your answer in the space provided.**

## Visiting a High-altitude City

A visitor to a city in Bolivia such as La Paz might find the following recommendations in a brochure in the hotel room:

*If it is your first day here in our lovely city, you must take it easy and rest. We recommend that you not walk for even short distances. You must not climb stairs.*

These recommendations are posted in hotel rooms to help warn visitors of the potential hazards of being at a high altitude. You see, La Paz is located at a high altitude in the Andes Mountains. People who are not used to living at such altitudes can contract *soroche,* or altitude sickness. Nausea, headaches, and tired muscles are some of the symptoms of this illness. These symptoms are caused by lack of oxygen from the thin air at high altitudes.

People who rent cars in La Paz are given containers of water to take with them. Car radiators quickly boil over in high altitudes, because water boils at a lower temperature in high altitudes than in low altitudes. Water needs to be replaced often in radiators of cars driven at high altitudes.

1. How do people get *soroche*?

(A) by driving too fast

(B) from resting the day they arrive in a city

(C) by buying it in a local store

(D) from too much activity the first few days in a high-altitude location

2. This article was written mainly to —

(F) explain the hazards of a high altitude.

(G) describe things to see in La Paz.

(H) welcome visitors to Bolivia.

(J) help you take care of rental cars.

3. Why should people who rent cars take containers of water with them?

_____

_____

_____

_____

_____

_____

**40**

# VISIONEAR

**The latest ALL-IN-ONE ENTERTAINMENT CENTER includes:**

- 27-inch television
- video recorder and player
- speaker phone
- personal computer

- CD player
- fax machine
- color printer

Other features include: remote control, 195 TV channels, and a superior sound system.

This Entertainment Center is the latest innovation in sight and sound. IT DOES EVERYTHING except pop your popcorn! You can actually cruise the Internet and talk to your friends on the speaker phone while you watch your favorite television program.

Many people already enjoy the convenience of VISIONEAR. You should be part of the "VISION" crowd and own one too! Imagine how people will look up to you because you were smart enough to be one of the FIRST people to own this superior Entertainment Center.

VISIONEAR is a quality product that everyone wants to own. We back this product with our 100% money-back guarantee, good for 40 days. NO IFS, ANDS, or BUTS. If you don't want it, we'll take it back. There is a small charge for restocking the product.

**GO ON**

**4.** This ad suggests that the Visionear —

Ⓐ  has advanced technology.

Ⓑ  has a popcorn popper.

Ⓒ  is inexpensive to purchase.

Ⓓ  is too heavy for one person to carry.

**5.** This ad was written mainly to tell about —

Ⓕ  the company that produces Visionear.

Ⓖ  the uses of a fax machine.

Ⓗ  a new home entertainment center.

Ⓙ  the cheapest television set for sale.

**6.** Which of these is an *opinion* in the ad?

Ⓐ  Other features include: remote control...

Ⓑ  You can actually cruise the Internet...

Ⓒ  Visionear is a quality product...

Ⓓ  There is a small charge for...

**7.** If you were asked to rename the Visionear, what would you call it? Why?

_____

_____

_____

_____

_____

**8.** The ad tries to appeal to your desire to —

Ⓕ  save the environment.

Ⓖ  be one of the first people to own the product.

Ⓗ  get good grades in school.

Ⓙ  travel to other countries and see new places.

**9.** There is enough information in this ad to show that Visionear —

Ⓐ  is a fairly new product.

Ⓑ  has been tested by a government agency.

Ⓒ  is not expensive.

Ⓓ  has an automatic shut-off system.

**10.** The Visionear has a money-back guarantee for —

Ⓕ  30 days.

Ⓖ  40 days.

Ⓗ  90 days.

Ⓙ  100 days.

**11.** What else would you like to add to the Visionear?

_____

_____

_____

_____

▶ GO ON

42

GO ON

## Sally Ride Makes History in Space

On June 18, 1983, Sally Ride became the first American woman to travel in space. She helped place three satellites over different parts of the world and conducted science experiments. But just as important as the scientific duties she performed, Ride showed a generation of girls that they could reach for the stars. The fields of science and space exploration were now open to women as well as men.

Sally Ride was born on May 26, 1951, in California. As a child her two favorite activities were sports and reading. She loved to play softball, football, and soccer. When she was about ten years old, she began to play tennis. She became one of the top junior tennis players in the country and was offered a tennis scholarship at a private high school in Los Angeles. It was there that she became truly interested in the field of science.

In college Sally Ride continued to play tennis and to study science. Her favorite subjects were astronomy and physics, and, after a few years, Sally also started taking English courses. She especially liked learning about Shakespeare. Sally Ride graduated from Stanford University in 1973 with degrees in English and physics. She continued graduate school at Stanford, combining her interests in physics and astronomy, and received a doctorate in *astrophysics.*

One day while Sally was looking for a job, she saw an advertisement from NASA (National Aeronautics and Space Administration) in the Stanford school paper. NASA was seeking applicants for a new space shuttle program. They were looking for engineers, scientists, and doctors to train as part of a group of astronauts, so Sally completed the forms and became one of the 208 finalists. The finalists were sent to the Johnson Space Center in Houston, Texas, where they were asked many questions. They were tested on how they would perform in an emergency situation. They also had to show that they were in good physical condition. Sally was thankful that she had always been physically active.

In January 1978, Sally Ride was selected to be one of the 35 astronaut candidates. The candidates moved to Houston for one year of training. If they successfully completed the training, they would have the opportunity to become astronauts. Sally's future husband, Steven Hawley, was also in this group. In 1979 both Ride and Hawley became astronauts.

In April 1982, Ride called her family and announced that she had been chosen as one of the astronauts for the seventh shuttle flight! The five astronauts worked closely together in a large office for the next year. They trained for the flight and learned to work together as a team.

On the day the space shuttle was to lift off, crowds of onlookers gathered along the Florida beaches to witness the launch. The mission went very smoothly and satellites were launched over Canada, Indonesia, and Germany. The flight lasted six days and made 98 orbits around the earth. When it touched down, Sally Ride had made history.

Core Skills Test Prep, Grade 7

**12.** Sally Ride became famous as the first —

(A) astronaut in space.

(B) woman in space.

(C) scientist in space.

(D) American woman in space.

**13.** Which of the following is an *opinion*?

(F) Sally Ride liked playing sports.

(G) Sally Ride became a valuable role model for girls.

(H) Sally Ride studied science in college.

(J) Sally Ride graduated from Stanford University in 1973.

**14.** In this selection the word *astrophysics* means —

(A) the study of marketing and advertising.

(B) the study of the way people lived in the past.

(C) the study of the physical and chemical nature of stars.

(D) the study of the human mind.

**15.** What was the first step Sally Ride took in becoming the first American woman to travel in space?

_____

_____

_____

_____

_____

**16.** This article would most likely be found in a book titled —

(F) *Famous Soccer Players.*

(G) *People Who Love Shakespeare.*

(H) *American Women in Space.*

(J) *Scientific Experiments in Space.*

**17.** How did Sally Ride's love of sports help her become an astronaut?

(A) Astronauts should play tennis well if they want to be successful.

(B) Participating in sports kept her in top physical condition.

(C) Only people who are very coordinated can become astronauts.

(D) All astronauts love sports.

**18.** Why did the five astronauts who were chosen for the seventh shuttle flight work together in one large office?

(F) NASA wanted all of the astronauts in the same room for security reasons.

(G) They needed to learn to work together.

(H) NASA didn't have much office space.

(J) They were all good friends and did not want separate offices.

**19.** If the author added a paragraph at the end of this selection, what would it include?

_____

_____

_____

_____

_____

▶**GO ON**

**44**

# Suffering from Allergies

Do you suffer from allergies? Did you know that more than forty million people in the United States have allergy problems? You may have heard the word *allergy* many times without knowing exactly what it means. An allergy is an unusual reaction to something that is harmless to most people. For example, if you have a ragweed allergy, you probably start sneezing whenever you are near ragweed. If you have a shellfish allergy, you might develop a rash if you eat lobster, shrimp, or crayfish.

People have probably had allergies throughout history. The paintings on the wall of an Egyptian ruler's tomb show that he died after being stung by a bee. This was a violent allergic reaction! Around A.D. 200 a Greek physician wrote about people sneezing when they were exposed to certain plants. Although allergies have existed for thousands of years, it was not until the mid-1800s that the medical community began to understand the causes and characteristics of allergies. At that time an English physician, W. R. Kirkman, collected the yellow dust called pollen from grasses he had grown. When he began to sneeze, he realized that he had discovered the cause of hay fever.

About the same time, another English doctor, Charles Blackley, developed an allergy test. He scratched one of his arms and put rye grass pollen on the cut. The scratch itched, swelled, and turned red. Blackley then scratched his other arm without adding pollen to the cut. Nothing happened. Blackley had the proof that he was allergic to rye grass. This test is called a scratch test, and it is still used today.

Our bodies protect us from germs and viruses by making substances called *antibodies*. Antibodies fight the germs and viruses that cause illness. An allergic reaction is really a mistake—the body mistakes something that is usually harmless, such as pollen, for a harmful invader. Special antibodies are produced and then the body releases a chemical that causes a runny nose, itchy skin, and sometimes, wheezing.

The material that produces an allergic reaction is called an allergen. Many allergens, such as mold, pollen, and mites, are present in the air. Mold is a small plant that grows in wet places. Mold spores are carried by the wind. Many grasses, weeds, and trees produce pollen that is carried by the wind. Mites are insects that are so small they cannot be seen. If you sneeze when the wind blows, you may be allergic to one of these things.

People can be allergic to many different things. Some people are allergic to certain foods. Their allergic reactions to these foods often include upset stomach, rashes, or breathing problems. Some foods that can cause allergic reactions are dairy products, wheat, corn, nuts, seafood, eggs, chocolate, and oranges.

Some people are allergic to drugs such as aspirin and penicillin, and other people are allergic to certain chemicals present in soaps and paints. Some people have allergic reactions when they are stung by bees or bitten by ants or mosquitoes. Doctors can help the allergy sufferer by prescribing pills, sprays, or nose drops. If these don't provide relief, doctors sometimes suggest allergy shots.

**20.** This selection would *most* likely be found in —

Ⓐ a travel guide to Greece.

Ⓑ an economics textbook.

Ⓒ a health magazine.

Ⓓ a world history textbook.

**21.** In an allergic reaction, the body mistakes an allergen for —

Ⓕ pollen.

Ⓖ an antibody.

Ⓗ a blood cell.

Ⓙ a harmful invader.

**22.** The third paragraph tells about —

Ⓐ the history of allergies.

Ⓑ the causes of allergies.

Ⓒ the development of the scratch test.

Ⓓ how to avoid allergies.

**23.** In the fourth paragraph, the word *antibodies* means —

Ⓕ germs blown in the wind.

Ⓖ viruses that attack the body.

Ⓗ substances the body makes to fight illness.

Ⓙ medicine given to allergy sufferers.

**24.** How do we know that people had allergies thousands of years ago?

_____

_____

_____

_____

**25.** All of the following phrases describe mold *except* —

Ⓐ it grows in wet places.

Ⓑ it protects us from viruses.

Ⓒ it is a small plant.

Ⓓ its spores are carried by the wind.

**26.** If you have hay fever, you will probably —

Ⓕ avoid fields when grasses are producing pollen.

Ⓖ use special soap to avoid getting a rash.

Ⓗ produce allergens.

Ⓙ avoid eating any dairy products.

**27.** If you sneeze when the wind blows you may be allergic to—

Ⓐ aspirin and penicillin.

Ⓑ mold, pollen, or mites.

Ⓒ chocolate or shellfish.

Ⓓ ants and bees.

**28.** Why do you think the author wrote this article?

_____

_____

_____

_____

_____

_____

_____

_____

▶**GO ON**▶

# A Visit to the Rain Forest

"I can't believe that you and I are both winners in the Amazon Rain Forest Adventure!" shouted Jess to her friend and fellow environmentalist.

"It is highly unusual for the government to choose two students from the same school for this educational journey. But we both worked hard on our science experiments, and our essays about why we wanted to go on this trip were chosen first and second in the state. Also, Mr. Hancock recommended both of us to the selection committee," Winnie responded with enthusiasm.

Jess and Winnie were both members of the school's Environmental Impact Committee (EIC). They made posters explaining the importance of the rain forests and how they provide Earth with forty percent of its oxygen supply by converting carbon dioxide into oxygen. Jess and Winnie also contacted speakers from the local university. These speakers conducted a school assembly showing the kinds of animals and plants that live in the rain forests and are in danger of becoming *extinct* as the rain forests disappear.

The girls' two-week trip to Brazil's Amazon Rain Forest started in Macapá, a city located at the mouth of the Amazon River. There were eight other students in their group. Four adults guided the students on a boat trip down the Amazon. During their journey they saw piranha (fish with razor-sharp teeth), alligators, monkeys, passion-fruit trees, and gorgeous flowers in every color imaginable. When the group reached Manaus they made themselves comfortable in a cabin near the river.

"The first night in the cabin was the most unforgettable. All night long I could hear the cries of animals in the rain forest, but of course I could see nothing because there were no lights near our cabin. I was nervous and afraid to sleep," said Winnie in her talk with her peers upon returning home from Brazil.

"I was so tired that first night from the exhaustion of canoeing for six hours that I slept very well," explained Jess.

"I was impressed with the difficult life of the people who live in the rain forest. They have none of the conveniences that we take for granted. They love the environment, though, and do not abuse it. I think this is partly because they are very dependent on their environment for the things they need to live," said Winnie.

"While I was in the rain forest enjoying its beauty and unique ecosystem, I thought about what I could do to help save this special place," said Jess. "I've decided to design a reusable container for use in grocery stores instead of grocery bags. This will lessen the number of trees cut down to make the bags. I hope to sell the bags to consumers and use the profits to buy as many acres of rain forest as possible," explained Jess.

**GO ON**

**29.** The description of the trip along the Amazon River helps you understand —

  (F) the work done by the university researchers.

  (G) the environment of a rain forest.

  (H) the enthusiasm the girls felt for their trip.

  (J) the rain forest at night.

**30.** In this selection, the word *extinct* means —

  (A) no longer existing.

  (B) no longer active.

  (C) no longer burning.

  (D) no longer being used.

**31.** The device the author uses in the first two paragraphs is —

  (F) suspense.

  (G) dialogue.

  (H) repetition.

  (J) flashback.

**32.** This selection would most likely be found in a book titled —

  (A) *Science Experiments*.

  (B) *School Assembly*.

  (C) *Educational Adventures*.

  (D) *The History of Recycling*.

**33.** Winnie explained why she was afraid the first night in the cabin so that —

  (F) her fellow students would understand how she felt.

  (G) Jess would admit that she too was afraid at night.

  (H) people would know why she did not like her trip.

  (J) her friends would be afraid to visit the rain forest.

**34.** Toward the end of the selection, how does Winnie feel about the people of the rain forest?

  _____

  _____

  _____

  _____

  _____

  _____

**35.** What does Jess decide to do to save the rain forest?

  _____

  _____

  _____

  _____

  _____

  _____

  _____

**STOP**

# Unit 4: Reading Vocabulary

## DETERMINING WORD MEANINGS

**Directions: Darken the circle for the word or group of words that has the same or almost the same meaning as the underlined word.**

| **Try This** | Choose your answer carefully. The other choices may seem correct. Be sure to think about the meaning of the underlined word. |
|---|---|

**Sample A**

To <u>link</u> means to —

Ⓐ separate.     Ⓒ clap.

Ⓑ join.     Ⓓ wash.

| **Think It Through** | The correct answer is B, join. <u>Link</u> means "join." <u>Link</u> does not mean separate, clap, or wash. |
|---|---|

---

1. To <u>amend</u> something is to —

   Ⓐ repeat it.     Ⓒ correct it.

   Ⓑ copy it.     Ⓓ save it.

2. To <u>meddle</u> is to —

   Ⓕ ignore.     Ⓗ knit.

   Ⓖ interfere.     Ⓙ avoid.

3. <u>Permanent</u> means —

   Ⓐ lasting.     Ⓒ pleasant.

   Ⓑ annoying.     Ⓓ temporary.

4. Something that is <u>witty</u> is —

   Ⓕ foolish.     Ⓗ boring.

   Ⓖ serious.     Ⓙ clever.

5. To <u>infuriate</u> is to make very —

   Ⓐ frightened.     Ⓒ safe.

   Ⓑ happy.     Ⓓ angry.

6. To <u>comply</u> is to —

   Ⓕ obey.     Ⓗ pretend.

   Ⓖ suspect.     Ⓙ admire.

7. An <u>intermission</u> is a kind of —

   Ⓐ pamphlet.     Ⓒ recess.

   Ⓑ errand.     Ⓓ competition.

8. A <u>hoax</u> is a kind of —

   Ⓕ box.     Ⓗ trick.

   Ⓖ candy.     Ⓙ rope.

9. To <u>cite</u> is to —

   Ⓐ look over.     Ⓒ speak for.

   Ⓑ find out.     Ⓓ refer to.

10. Something that is <u>profound</u> is —

   Ⓕ deep.     Ⓗ easy.

   Ⓖ stupid.     Ⓙ shallow.

**STOP**

# MATCHING WORDS WITH MORE THAN ONE MEANING

**Directions:** Darken the circle for the sentence that uses the underlined word in the same way as the sentence in the box.

| **Try This** | Read the sentence in the box. Decide what the underlined word means. Then find the answer choice in which the underlined word has the same meaning. |
| --- | --- |

**Sample A**

> We made a <u>fast</u> exit from the crowded gym.

In which sentence does <u>fast</u> have the same meaning as it does in the sentence above?

Ⓐ The <u>fast</u> current washed the pier away.

Ⓑ The clock in the hall is running <u>fast</u>.

Ⓒ The baby was <u>fast</u> asleep in a crib.

Ⓓ You must <u>fast</u> before medical tests.

**STOP**

| **Think It Through** | The correct answer is A. In choice A and in the sentence in the box, <u>fast</u> means "moving quickly." |
| --- | --- |

**1.**

> Our team won first <u>place</u> in the race.

In which sentence does <u>place</u> have the same meaning as it does in the sentence above?

Ⓐ <u>Place</u> the bowl carefully on the table.

Ⓑ The beach is a quiet <u>place</u> to relax.

Ⓒ Which <u>place</u> at the table is yours?

Ⓓ Don't worry if you finish in last <u>place</u>.

**2.**

> The actor forgot his opening <u>line</u>.

In which sentence does <u>line</u> have the same meaning as it does in the sentence above?

Ⓕ Don't cross the yellow <u>line</u> on a highway.

Ⓖ We had to stand in <u>line</u> to get movie tickets.

Ⓗ Can you rewrite the last <u>line</u>?

Ⓙ The children will <u>line</u> up to go outside.

**3.**

> We'll all do our <u>part</u> on the project.

In which sentence does <u>part</u> have the same meaning as it does in the sentence above?

Ⓐ Which <u>part</u> of the city is the oldest?

Ⓑ Ben wants a <u>part</u> in the school play.

Ⓒ I replaced a broken <u>part</u> on my car.

Ⓓ Isabel won't <u>part</u> with her hat.

**4.**

> Small <u>craft</u> are in danger in storms.

In which sentence does <u>craft</u> have the same meaning as it does in the sentence above?

Ⓕ The cat showed great <u>craft</u> in catching the mouse.

Ⓖ Sam can <u>craft</u> many things from wood.

Ⓗ Sailing <u>craft</u> of all types filled the harbor.

Ⓙ Weaving is an ancient <u>craft</u>.

**STOP**

# USING CONTEXT CLUES

**Directions:** Darken the circle for the word or words that give the meaning of the underlined word, or write your answer in the space provided.

| Try This | Read the first sentence carefully. Look for clue words in the sentence. Then use each answer choice in place of the underlined word. Be sure that your answer and the underlined word have the same meaning. |
|---|---|

**Sample A**

The <u>dismal</u> weather has been cold and rainy for days. <u>Dismal</u> means —

- Ⓐ bright.
- Ⓒ windy.
- Ⓑ gloomy.
- Ⓓ changeable.

| Think It Through | The correct answer is B. <u>Dismal</u> means "gloomy." The clue words are "cold" and "rainy." All four choices have something to do with weather. But only <u>gloomy</u> has the same meaning as <u>dismal</u>. |
|---|---|

1. Miriam was <u>dubious</u> about her chances of winning. <u>Dubious</u> means —
   - Ⓐ positive.
   - Ⓒ doubtful.
   - Ⓑ hopeful.
   - Ⓓ happy.

2. The <u>sapling</u> had to be watered twice a day. A <u>sapling</u> is a —
   - Ⓕ large bush.
   - Ⓗ species of tropical bird.
   - Ⓖ young tree.
   - Ⓙ type of rose.

3. The stream <u>receded</u> after the rains stopped. <u>Receded</u> means —
   - Ⓐ withdrew.
   - Ⓒ overflowed.
   - Ⓑ flowed.
   - Ⓓ flooded.

4. The baby sitter tried to quiet the <u>boisterous</u> children. <u>Boisterous</u> means —

   _____

   _____

5. The student included many details and gave an <u>accurate</u> summary of the story. <u>Accurate</u> means —
   - Ⓕ exaggerated.
   - Ⓗ poor.
   - Ⓖ exact.
   - Ⓙ partial.

6. Painting is a <u>tedious</u> task because you must work slowly and carefully. <u>Tedious</u> means —
   - Ⓐ painful.
   - Ⓒ boring.
   - Ⓑ creative.
   - Ⓓ interesting.

7. The patient suffered <u>acute</u> pain from his injuries. <u>Acute</u> means —
   - Ⓕ frequent.
   - Ⓗ intense.
   - Ⓖ slight.
   - Ⓙ mild.

8. The charity had a fund-raiser to <u>generate</u> money for its projects. <u>Generate</u> means —

   _____

   _____

**STOP**

# Test

**Sample A**

To <u>motivate</u> is to —

Ⓐ discourage.

Ⓑ work.

Ⓒ accept.

Ⓓ inspire.

**For questions 1–9, darken the circle for the word or group of words that has the same or almost the same meaning as the underlined word.**

1. A <u>boulevard</u> is a kind of —

   Ⓐ building.

   Ⓑ watch.

   Ⓒ street.

   Ⓓ museum.

2. An <u>abyss</u> is a —

   Ⓕ crater.

   Ⓖ movie.

   Ⓗ kind of dress.

   Ⓙ fruit.

3. <u>Vacant</u> means —

   Ⓐ colorful.

   Ⓑ fresh.

   Ⓒ occupied.

   Ⓓ empty.

4. A <u>jaunt</u> is —

   Ⓕ an experience.

   Ⓖ an outing.

   Ⓗ a problem.

   Ⓙ an opportunity.

5. To <u>convey</u> is to —

   Ⓐ build.

   Ⓑ transport.

   Ⓒ examine.

   Ⓓ memorize.

6. A <u>boutique</u> is a kind of —

   Ⓕ store.

   Ⓖ designer.

   Ⓗ show.

   Ⓙ florist.

7. To <u>recollect</u> is to —

   Ⓐ remember.

   Ⓑ watch.

   Ⓒ forget.

   Ⓓ bargain.

8. Someone who is <u>optimistic</u> is —

   Ⓕ discouraged.

   Ⓖ hopeful.

   Ⓗ sad.

   Ⓙ funny.

9. To <u>collapse</u> means to —

   Ⓐ fall down.

   Ⓑ go around.

   Ⓒ sell out.

   Ⓓ blow up.

**GO ON**

Name _____    Date _____

**Sample B**

There are costumes in the old <u>trunk</u>.

In which sentence does <u>trunk</u> have the same meaning as it does in the sentence above?

Ⓐ The baby elephant raised its <u>trunk</u>.

Ⓑ Two squirrels ran down the tree <u>trunk</u>.

Ⓒ Put these boxes in the <u>trunk</u> of my car.

Ⓓ Grandmother's <u>trunk</u> is in the basement.

For questions 10–13, darken the circle for the sentence in which the underlined word means the same as it does in the sentence in the box.

**10.**

Will the town <u>recover</u> from the storm damage?

In which sentence does <u>recover</u> have the same meaning as it does in the sentence above?

Ⓕ Jill got some fabric to <u>recover</u> the cushion.

Ⓖ I will <u>recover</u> from the accident soon.

Ⓗ Will the police <u>recover</u> the stolen property?

Ⓙ Those recyling companies <u>recover</u> steel from old appliances.

**11.**

Does Matt exercise to stay <u>fit</u>?

In which sentence does <u>fit</u> have the same meaning as it does in the sentence above?

Ⓐ My clothes don't <u>fit</u> since I've grown.

Ⓑ Will that table <u>fit</u> here?

Ⓒ You need to be <u>fit</u> to enter that race.

Ⓓ Shoes that don't <u>fit</u> properly can hurt.

**12.**

A flood can <u>sweep</u> away everything in its path.

In which sentence does <u>sweep</u> have the same meaning as it does in the sentence above?

Ⓕ Our track team will <u>sweep</u> all the events.

Ⓖ Can you <u>sweep</u> aside your doubts?

Ⓗ Karl will <u>sweep</u> the gym floors.

Ⓙ The famous actress likes to <u>sweep</u> into a room.

**13.**

Her clothes were in a <u>mess</u> on the floor.

In which sentence does <u>mess</u> have the same meaning as it does in the sentence above?

Ⓐ I'll clean up this <u>mess</u> before I leave.

Ⓑ Please don't <u>mess</u> with my things!

Ⓒ She'll <u>mess</u> this up if she is in a hurry.

Ⓓ The soldiers met in the <u>mess</u> tent.

**14.**

Dad will <u>hang</u> the painting for me.

Write a new sentence in which <u>hang</u> has the same meaning as it does in the sentence above.

_____

_____

_____

_____

_____

_____

**GO ON▶**

Unit 4
Core Skills Test Prep, Grade 7

**Sample C**

We camped in the grotto under the cliffs. A grotto is —

Ⓐ a group of trees.

Ⓑ a small cave.

Ⓒ a simple hut.

Ⓓ a forest preserve.

**STOP**

**For questions 15–20, darken the circle for the word or words that give the meaning of the underlined word.**

15. It has been an extremely brutal winter with very cold temperatures. Brutal means —

Ⓐ harsh.

Ⓑ windy.

Ⓒ gentle.

Ⓓ pleasant.

16. Brass is an alloy of copper and zinc. An alloy is —

Ⓕ a type of plastic.

Ⓖ a mixture of metals.

Ⓗ a kind of sword.

Ⓙ a kind of ore.

17. The two interstate highways run in different directions, but they intersect in Atlanta. Intersect means —

Ⓐ end.

Ⓑ run parallel.

Ⓒ cross each other.

Ⓓ begin.

18. She offered a feeble excuse for her tardiness, but she could tell we didn't believe it. Feeble means —

Ⓕ truthful.       Ⓗ exaggerated.

Ⓖ excellent.       Ⓙ weak.

19. That sofa was manufactured in our new furniture factory. Manufactured means —

Ⓐ sold.       Ⓒ made.

Ⓑ designed.       Ⓓ used.

20. Brad took Jana's arm and escorted her down the runway. Escorted means —

Ⓕ accompanied.

Ⓖ led.

Ⓗ followed.

Ⓙ carried.

**Write the following meanings:**

21. Because Gerardo is organized and efficient, he is a capable office manager. Capable means —

_____

_____

_____

_____

22. Marta smiled when she heard the joyful clamor coming from the playroom. Clamor means —

_____

_____

_____

_____

**STOP**

# Unit 5: Math Problem-Solving Strategies

## OVERVIEW
## The Problem-Solving Plan

*When solving math problems follow these steps:*

**STEP 1:**  **WHAT IS THE QUESTION/GOAL?**

Read the problem.  Decide what must be found.  This is sometimes in the form of a question.

**STEP 2:**  **FIND THE FACTS**

Locate the factual information in three different ways:

    **A.**  KEY FACTS...the facts you need to solve the problem.

    **B.**  FACTS YOU DON'T NEED...those facts that are not necessary for solving the problem.

    **C.**  ARE MORE FACTS NEEDED?...decide if you have enough information to solve the problem.

**STEP 3:**  **SELECT A STRATEGY**

Decide what strategies you might use, how you will use them, and then estimate what your answer will be. If one strategy does not help solve the problem, try another.

**STEP 4:**  **SOLVE**

Apply the strategy according to your plan. Use an operation if necessary, and clearly indicate your answer.

**STEP 5:**  **DOES YOUR RESPONSE MAKE SENSE?**

Write your answer in a complete sentence.  Read the problem again.  Check to see that your answer makes sense.  Use estimation to check calculations.

# PROBLEM 1

**PROBLEM/QUESTION:**

Justine drives to her company's main office every day, Monday through Thursday. The trip is 20 miles one way. On Friday, she drives to the regional office. This trip is 50 miles one way. How many miles does Justine drive in three weeks?

**STEP 1: WHAT IS THE QUESTION/GOAL?**

**STEP 2: FIND THE FACTS**

**STEP 3: SELECT A STRATEGY**

**STEP 4: SOLVE**

**STEP 5: DOES YOUR RESPONSE MAKE SENSE?**

Core Skills Test Prep, Grade 7

# PROBLEM 2

**PROBLEM/QUESTION:**

Ian began the week with $48. On Monday, he spent half of it. On Tuesday, he spent one-third of the amount he still had. On Wednesday, he spent one fourth of the money he still had. On Thursday, he spent one-sixth of the amount he still had. On what day did he spend the most money?

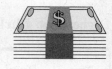

**STEP 1:   WHAT IS THE QUESTION/GOAL?**

**STEP 2:   FIND THE FACTS**

**STEP 3:   SELECT A STRATEGY**

**STEP 4:   SOLVE**

**STEP 5:   DOES YOUR RESPONSE MAKE SENSE?**

Name _____  Date _____

# Unit 6: Math Problem Solving and Procedures

## UNDERSTANDING NUMBER RELATIONSHIPS

**Directions: Darken the circle for the correct answer, or write it in the space provided.**

| **Try This** | Read each problem carefully. Make sure you understand the question that is being asked. Then choose the best method to solve the problem. |
|---|---|

**Sample A**

Which fraction is smallest in value?

Ⓐ $\frac{1}{8}$          Ⓒ $\frac{3}{5}$

Ⓑ $\frac{1}{5}$          Ⓓ $\frac{3}{8}$

| **Think It Through** | The correct answer is <u>A</u>. The fraction $\frac{1}{8}$ is smaller than the other fractions listed. Using the common denominator 40, $\frac{1}{8}$ becomes $\frac{5}{40}$, and the other fractions become $\frac{8}{40}$, $\frac{24}{40}$, and $\frac{15}{40}$. |
|---|---|

1. What is the value of point X on the number line?

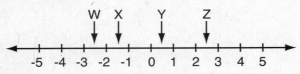

Ⓐ 0.5          Ⓒ −1.5

Ⓑ 2.5          Ⓓ −2.5

2. Each represents 0.01.

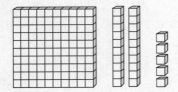

Which decimal is shown by the figure above?

Ⓕ 1.25

Ⓖ 12.5

Ⓗ 0.0125

Ⓙ 120.5

3. After picking berries, 4 friends compared the amounts of berries in their buckets. Juan's bucket was $\frac{2}{3}$ full, Jamie's bucket was $\frac{4}{5}$ full, Lenny's bucket was $\frac{3}{4}$ full, and Hazel's bucket was $\frac{3}{8}$ full. How would these amounts be arranged in order from greatest to least?

Ⓐ $\frac{4}{5}, \frac{3}{4}, \frac{2}{3}, \frac{3}{8}$          Ⓒ $\frac{3}{8}, \frac{3}{4}, \frac{4}{5}, \frac{2}{3}$

Ⓑ $\frac{2}{3}, \frac{3}{4}, \frac{3}{8}, \frac{4}{5}$          Ⓓ $\frac{3}{8}, \frac{2}{3}, \frac{4}{5}, \frac{3}{4}$

4. The thermometer shows the reading early this morning. By noon, the temperature had increased 15° from the early morning reading. What is the new reading?

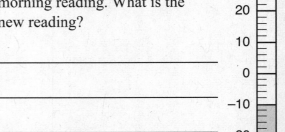

_____

_____

_____

# UNDERSTANDING NUMBER THEORY

**Directions: Darken the circle for the correct answer, or write it in the space provided.**

| **Try This** | Read the question twice before choosing your answer. Make sure you understand the question that is being asked. Think about which numbers stand for ones, tens, hundreds, and so on. |
|---|---|

## Sample A

The call number on this library book is 612.48. What is the value of the 8 in this number?

Ⓐ 8 ten-thousandths

Ⓑ 8 thousandths

Ⓒ 8 hundredths

Ⓓ 8 tenths

> 612.48  Remembering Vietnam/Quy Luong
> L        Luong, Quy
>          Illustrations by Thuy Dang
>          San Francisco: Freedom Rings Press,
>          1990
>          147 p. : ill. ; 23 cm.
>          1. Vietnam. I. Luong, Quy. II. Title

| **Think It Through** | The correct answer is C. In the number 612.48, the 8 is in the hundredths place, so its value is 8 hundredths. The 4 is in the tenths place. |
|---|---|

1. Which of these means the same as $5^3$?

   Ⓐ 15      Ⓒ 8

   Ⓑ 125     Ⓓ 243

2. One estimate for the distance from Earth to the Andromeda Galaxy is 2,300,000 light years. What is this distance expressed in scientific notation?

   Ⓕ $2.3 \times 10^5$      Ⓗ $2.3 \times 10^6$

   Ⓖ $23 \times 10^5$       Ⓙ $23 \times 10^7$

3. How would the product $3 \times 3 \times 7 \times 5 \times 5$ be expressed in exponential notation?

   Ⓐ $3^3 \times 7 \times 5^5$

   Ⓑ $2^3$

   Ⓒ $3^2 \times 7 \times 5^2$

   Ⓓ $10^5$

4. Look at the factor tree shown here. Notice the number of branches in the factor tree.

   How many branches will the number 17 have in its completed factor tree?

   _____

   _____

   _____

# WORKING WITH ALGEBRA

**Directions: Darken the circle for the correct answer, or write in your answer.**

| Try This | Check your work by making sure both sides of an equation are equal values. Try using all the answer choices in the problem to help you choose the correct solution. |
|---|---|

## Sample A

Which value of x makes the equation
$x - 12 = 40$ correct?

Ⓐ 60      Ⓒ 45

Ⓑ 52      Ⓓ 38

| Think It Through | The correct answer is <u>B</u>, <u>52</u>. Because the unknown number minus 12 equals 40, it is necessary to add 40 and 12 to find the unknown. |
|---|---|

1. Meg baked a chocolate cake. She knows that the cake contains 2,700 calories. She has cut the cake into 12 equal-sized pieces. If $c$ represents the number of calories in one piece, which equation can she use to find the number of calories in each piece?

   Ⓐ $12 + c = 2,700$

   Ⓑ $12 \div c = 2,700$

   Ⓒ $12c = 2,700$

   Ⓓ $2700 - c = 12$

2. What is another way to write $6(a + 7)$?

   Ⓕ $(6 + a) \times (6 + 7)$

   Ⓖ $6a + 7$

   Ⓗ $7 \times (6 + a)$

   Ⓙ $(6 \times a) + (6 \times 7)$

3. It took Gene three times as long to paint one side of the fence as it took David to paint the other side. If h is the number of hours David painted, which expression shows the time spent by Gene painting?

   Ⓐ $3 \times h$

   Ⓑ $3 - h$

   Ⓒ $3 + h$

   Ⓓ $3 \div h$

4. Which of the following problems could be solved by the equation $2x = 36 + 52$?

   Ⓕ Greg has 36 trading cards. Harry has twice as many. How many cards does Harry have?

   Ⓖ Class A has 36 students, and Class B has twice as many as 52 students. How many more students are in Class B?

   Ⓗ The first plant is 36 inches tall, and the second plant is 52 inches tall. If their heights were doubled, how tall would they each be?

   Ⓙ Tank A has 36 fish, and Tank B has 52 fish. If the fish are divided equally between both tanks, how many fish will be in each tank?

5. Clara's pay from her paper route is based on the expression $\$15 + \$0.10p$, where $p$ is the number of papers she delivers during the week. What would her weekly pay be if she delivers 315 papers each week?

   _____

   _____

**STOP**

**60**

# UNDERSTANDING PATTERNS AND FUNCTIONS

**Directions: Darken the circle for the correct answer, or write in the answer.**

| Try This | Read each question carefully. Determine the nature of the pattern or relationship in the problem. Try using all the answer choices in the problem. Then choose the answer that you think best answers the question. |
|---|---|

**Sample A**

Look at the pattern shown here. Which number is missing?

101, 105, 109, ☐, 117

Ⓐ 113     Ⓒ 110

Ⓑ 112     Ⓓ 107

| Think It Through | The correct answer is <u>A</u>. The pattern shows that each number increases by 4. Therefore, to find the missing number, add 109 and 4 to get the answer, <u>113</u>. |
|---|---|

---

1. A special machine changes numbers according to a certain rule. The *out* number in the table shows the result when the rule is applied to the *in* number.

| In | 5 | 45 | 20 |
|---|---|---|---|
| Out | 1 | 9 | 4 |

What number will 30 be changed to?

Ⓐ 150

Ⓑ 35

Ⓒ 25

Ⓓ 6

2. In a basketball free-throw contest held at the high school, Rudy made 4 out of 5 free throws. At this rate, how many free throws could he expect to make in 25 tries?

_____

_____

_____

3. Fran bought 6 yards of blue tapestry material. She used it to upholster 3 chairs. How much of the material would she need to upholster 7 chairs?

Ⓕ 21 yards

Ⓖ 16 yards

Ⓗ 14 yards

Ⓙ 10 yards

4. Shown here are the first three figures in a pattern. How many stars would be in the seventh figure of the pattern?

Ⓐ 20

Ⓑ 23

Ⓒ 26

Ⓓ 28

Unit 5
Core Skills Test Prep, Grade 7

# WORKING WITH PROBABILITY AND STATISTICS

**Directions: Darken the circle for the correct answer, or write in the answer.**

| Try This | Read each question twice before choosing your answer. Study any given tables or graphs to help you choose the correct answer. |
|---|---|

**Sample A**

Two pennies are tossed into the air. What is the probability they will match either heads-heads or tails-tails when they land?

(A) $\frac{1}{1}$   (C) $\frac{1}{4}$

(B) $\frac{1}{2}$   (D) $\frac{1}{8}$

| Think It Through | The correct answer is B. There are four possible outcomes: heads-heads, tails-tails, heads-tails, and tails-heads. Two of these four possibilities will match. That makes the correct answer a probability of $\frac{2}{4}$, or $\frac{1}{2}$. |
|---|---|

1. Two six-sided number cubes, each numbered 1 through 6, are rolled together. What is the probability that they will land with the numbers on the top face having a sum greater than 10?

(A) 1 out of 6

(B) 1 out of 12

(C) 2 out of 36

(D) 10 out of 30

2. These are Yung's bowling scores for the past month.

| | | |
|---|---|---|
| 192 | 148 | 192 |
| 150 | 175 | 202 |
| 269 | 225 | 240 |
| 148 | 121 | 192 |

What is Yung's bowling average rounded to the nearest whole number?

3. According to this graph, which two energy sources together account for nearly one half?

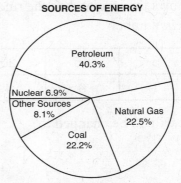

SOURCES OF ENERGY

Petroleum 40.3%
Nuclear 6.9%
Other Sources 8.1%
Natural Gas 22.5%
Coal 22.2%

(F) nuclear and natural gas

(G) coal and other sources

(H) petroleum and coal

(J) natural gas and coal

4. Helen has a choice of 3 colors of paint, 4 kinds of curtains, and 2 colors of carpet to decorate her apartment. How many different combinations of paint, curtains, and carpets can she use?

(A) 9   (C) 24

(B) 18   (D) 36

**GO ON**

Miguel earned $20 at his part-time job. The following graph shows how he spent the money. Study the graph. Then answer questions 5 and 6.

**Miguel's Earnings**

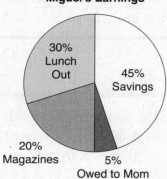

**5.** What percent of his money did Miguel spend on lunch and magazines combined?

(F) 50%          (H) 20%

(G) 30%          (J) 25%

**6.** Which tally chart shows the data in the circle graph?

(A)

| Lunch | 𝖳𝖧𝖫 𝖳𝖧𝖫 𝖳𝖧𝖫 𝖳𝖧𝖫 |
|---|---|
| Magazines | 𝖳𝖧𝖫 𝖳𝖧𝖫 𝖳𝖧𝖫 𝖳𝖧𝖫 𝖳𝖧𝖫 𝖳𝖧𝖫 |
| Owed | 𝖳𝖧𝖫 |
| Savings | 𝖳𝖧𝖫 𝖳𝖧𝖫 𝖳𝖧𝖫 𝖳𝖧𝖫 𝖳𝖧𝖫 𝖳𝖧𝖫 𝖳𝖧𝖫 𝖳𝖧𝖫 𝖳𝖧𝖫 |

(B)

| Lunch | 𝖳𝖧𝖫 𝖳𝖧𝖫 𝖳𝖧𝖫 𝖳𝖧𝖫 𝖳𝖧𝖫 |
|---|---|
| Magazines | 𝖳𝖧𝖫 𝖳𝖧𝖫 𝖳𝖧𝖫 𝖳𝖧𝖫 |
| Owed | 𝖳𝖧𝖫 |
| Savings | 𝖳𝖧𝖫 𝖳𝖧𝖫 𝖳𝖧𝖫 𝖳𝖧𝖫 𝖳𝖧𝖫 𝖳𝖧𝖫 𝖳𝖧𝖫 𝖳𝖧𝖫 𝖳𝖧𝖫 |

(C)

| Lunch | 𝖳𝖧𝖫 𝖳𝖧𝖫 𝖳𝖧𝖫 |
|---|---|
| Magazines | 𝖳𝖧𝖫 𝖳𝖧𝖫 |
| Owed | 𝖳𝖧𝖫 |
| Savings | 𝖳𝖧𝖫 𝖳𝖧𝖫 𝖳𝖧𝖫 𝖳𝖧𝖫 𝖳𝖧𝖫 |

(D)

| Lunch | 𝖳𝖧𝖫 𝖳𝖧𝖫 𝖳𝖧𝖫 𝖳𝖧𝖫 |
|---|---|
| Magazines | 𝖳𝖧𝖫 𝖳𝖧𝖫 𝖳𝖧𝖫 𝖳𝖧𝖫 𝖳𝖧𝖫 |
| Owed | 𝖳𝖧𝖫 |
| Savings | 𝖳𝖧𝖫 𝖳𝖧𝖫 𝖳𝖧𝖫 𝖳𝖧𝖫 𝖳𝖧𝖫 |

The graph below shows the prices of two stocks over a period of time. Use the graph to answer questions 7–9.

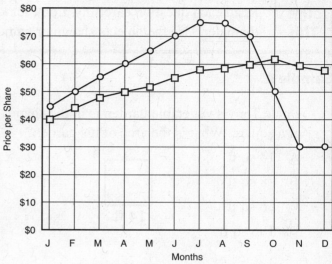

**7.** What was the greatest price difference between Abbott and Claney stock during the period shown on the graph?

(F) $30          (H) $19

(G) $27          (J) $15

**8.** Ella bought 20 shares of Claney stock in April and sold them in October at the current price at that time. About how much profit did she make?

(A) About $100

(B) About $220

(C) About $285

(D) About $325

**9.** If Larry bought 12 shares of Abbott stock on May 4, what did he pay for the stock?

_____

_____

# UNDERSTANDING GEOMETRY

**Directions: Darken the circle for the correct answer, or write in the answer.**

| **Try This** | Read each question carefully. Look for key words such as <u>area</u>, <u>volume</u>, <u>radius</u>, and <u>diameter</u>. Use the objects shown or named to help you answer each question. |
|---|---|

**Sample A**

Uncle Tony's vegetable garden is in the shape of a square. What is the area of his garden?

Ⓐ  14 sq ft

Ⓑ  28 sq ft

Ⓒ  56 sq ft

Ⓓ  196 sq ft

**14 ft**

| **Think It Through** | The correct answer is <u>D, 196 sq ft</u>. To determine the area of a square, multiply side by side: $A = s \times s$. So, $14 \times 14 = 196$. |
|---|---|

**STOP**

---

1. Michiko's mother stores buttons in the box shown here. What is the volume of the box? (Use $V = l \times w \times h$.)

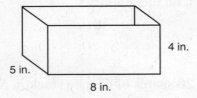
4 in.
5 in.
8 in.

Ⓐ  160 cu in.

Ⓑ  80 cu in.

Ⓒ  73 cu in.

Ⓓ  17 cu in.

2. An ice-skating rink is shown here. What is the area of the rink? (Use $A = lw$.)

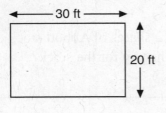
← 30 ft →
20 ft

_____

_____

3. Rectangle FGDE is similar to rectangle ECBA. Which line segments are perpendicular?

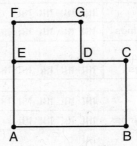

Ⓕ  $\overline{FG}$ and $\overline{DC}$

Ⓖ  $\overline{AB}$ and $\overline{ED}$

Ⓗ  $\overline{EA}$ and $\overline{AB}$

Ⓙ  $\overline{CB}$ and $\overline{FE}$

4. An apple pie has a diameter of 9 inches. What is its circumference rounded to the nearest whole number? (Use $C = \pi d$ and $\pi = 3.14$.)

Ⓐ  14 inches

Ⓑ  28 inches

Ⓒ  36 inches

Ⓓ  57 inches

**GO ON**

Name _____    Date _____

**5.** Which of these angles appears to be an obtuse angle?

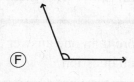 F

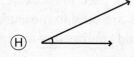 G

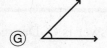 H

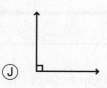 J

**6.** Which transformation moves the figure from position A to position B?

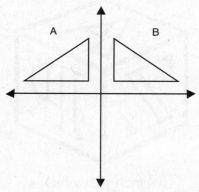

Ⓐ rotation   Ⓒ reflection
Ⓑ translation   Ⓓ extension

**7.** The diameter of this circle is represented by which line segment?

Ⓕ $\overline{XA}$
Ⓖ $\overline{XC}$
Ⓗ $\overline{BX}$
Ⓙ $\overline{AC}$

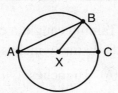

**8.** Which of these pattern pieces would *not* form a cube if folded along the dotted lines?

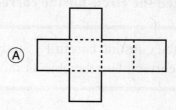 A

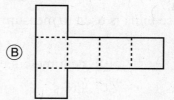 B

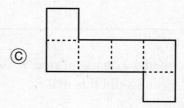 C

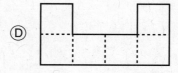 D

**9.** The distance from the edge to the center of a circle is called the —

_____
_____
_____
_____
_____
_____

# WORKING WITH MEASUREMENT

**Directions: Darken the circle for the correct answer, or write the answer in the space provided.**

| Try This | Read the question carefully. Study the answer choices. Sometimes more than one answer looks correct. Use the objects shown or named to help you answer each question. |
|---|---|

**Sample A**

Which of these units is used to measure length on a ruler?

(A) degrees     (C) centimeters

(B) kilograms     (D) liters

| Think It Through | The correct answer is <u>C</u>. Degrees are used to measure temperature, kilograms are used to measure mass, liters are used to measure capacity, and <u>centimeters</u> are used to measure length. |
|---|---|

1. Mr. Baker cooked $4\frac{1}{2}$ quarts of rice. How many 1-cup servings did this make?

   (A) $5\frac{1}{2}$ cups

   (B) 9 cups

   (C) 10 cups

   (D) 18 cups

2. The scale model shown here represents a rectangular parking lot.

Scale: 1cm represents 15m

Use your centimeter ruler to help answer this question. What is the actual length of each of the 2 long sides of the parking lot?

   (F) 4 meters

   (G) 15 meters

   (H) 60 meters

   (J) 90 meters

3. Use your inch ruler to help answer this question. What is the approximate length of one side of this toy block?

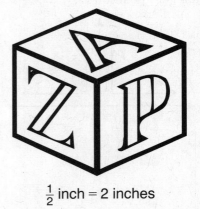

$\frac{1}{2}$ inch = 2 inches

_____

_____

_____

4. Tammy caught a catfish that was $2\frac{2}{3}$ feet long. How many inches long was it?

   (A) 16 inches     (C) 29 inches

   (B) 26 inches     (D) 32 inches

**GO ON**

**66**

**5.** How high off the ground is the kite?

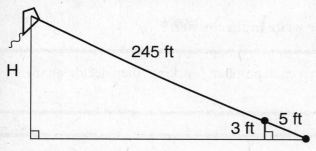

- Ⓕ 300 feet
- Ⓖ 245 feet
- Ⓗ 150 feet
- Ⓙ 145 feet

**6.** The testing session began at 8:45 A.M. The time limit on the first test was 35 minutes and the time limit on the second test was 40 minutes. There was a 10-minute break between the tests. At what time did the session end?

- Ⓐ 10:00 A.M.
- Ⓑ 10:10 A.M.
- Ⓒ 10:25 A.M.
- Ⓓ 11:05 A.M.

**7.** Gino and Claire went to see a movie last night. The movie began at 7:30 P.M. It lasted $1\frac{3}{4}$ hours. What time did the movie end?

- Ⓕ 9:15 P.M.
- Ⓖ 9:20 P.M.
- Ⓗ 9:30 P.M.
- Ⓙ 9:45 P.M.

**8.** On a map of a cross-country ski area, 1 inch represents 3 miles. What is the distance between two turn-around areas 4 inches apart on the map?

- Ⓐ 3 miles
- Ⓑ 4 miles
- Ⓒ 7 miles
- Ⓓ 12 miles

**9.** The picture shows that Miyoshi is standing 6 yards from the tree. How many feet is that?

6 yards between girl and tree

_____
_____
_____
_____
_____
_____

**10.** Marty's soccer team starts its practice at 4:30 P.M. It ends at 5:15 P.M. How long does Marty's soccer team practice?

_____
_____
_____

STOP

**67**

Name _____ Date _____

# USING PROBLEM-SOLVING STRATEGIES

**Directions: Darken the circle for the correct answer, or write in the answer.**

| Try This | Study each problem carefully. Think about what each problem is asking, then decide on the best strategy to find the answer. |
|---|---|

**Sample A**

A local factory produces tuners for car radios. Of the 400 tuners produced each hour, 30 are damaged. How many undamaged tuners does the factory produce in an 8-hour day?

Ⓐ 370          Ⓒ 2,960

Ⓑ 430          Ⓓ 3,440

| Think It Through | The correct answer is C, 2,960. If 30 out of 400 produced each hour are damaged, then 370 are undamaged. To find how many undamaged tuners are produced in 8 hours, multiply 370 times 8 to get 2,960. |
|---|---|

STOP

1. Joyce decorated a tree in her yard with popcorn for birds to eat. On the first branch, she hung a string with 4 pieces of popcorn. On the second branch, she hung a string with 8 pieces of popcorn, and on the third branch a string with 16 pieces of popcorn. If she continued this pattern, how many pieces of popcorn would be on the string that she hung on the fifth branch?

Ⓐ 18          Ⓒ 32

Ⓑ 24          Ⓓ 64

2. During the first three hours at the car wash, 15 fewer cars were washed during the first hour than during the third hour. During the second hour, 5 more cars were washed than during the first hour. During the third hour, 40 cars were washed. How many cars were washed during the second hour?

_____

_____

3. Frances wants to provide each of her students with 5 strips of leather for an art project. She buys the leather strips at a craft store for $0.89 each. What other information is needed to learn how much Frances pays for the leather strips?

Ⓕ the length of each strip

Ⓖ the number of students in her class

Ⓗ the number of strips in a package

Ⓙ the colors of strips available

**Use the figure shown here to answer question 4.**

| | | | | | |
|---|---|---|---|---|---|
| | | | | 12 | Row 1 |
| | | | 14 | 16 | Row 2 |
| | | 18 | 20 | 22 | Row 3 |
| | 24 | 26 | 28 | 30 | Row 4 |
| 32 | 34 | 36 | 38 | 40 | Row 5 |
| | | | | | Row 6 |

4. Fill in the numbers to complete Row 6.

STOP

**68**

Name _____ Date _____

# USING ESTIMATION

**Directions: Darken the circle for the correct answer, or write in the answer.**

<table>
<tr><td>**Try This**</td><td>Round numbers when you estimate. For some problems, there are no exact answers. Then you should take your best guess. You can check your answer by using the numbers given in the problem.</td></tr>
</table>

**Sample A**

Lucas bought 3 magazines: one for $3.25, one for $2.75, and one for $4.57. With tax included, about how much did Lucas spend?

Ⓐ $9     Ⓒ $13

Ⓑ $11     Ⓓ $15

<table>
<tr><td>**Think It Through**</td><td>The correct answer is <u>B</u>, $11.00. Round $3.25 to $3.00, $2.75 to $3.00, and $4.57 to $5.00. The sum of these estimates is $11.00, which would include about $0.80 in tax. Check by adding $3.25, $2.75, $4.57 and $0.80. The sum is $11.37.</td></tr>
</table>

**STOP**

1. Terri is working on a class project. She cut a pine board into 12 equal parts. She used 9 of the pieces to build some shelves. About what percent of the board is left?

Ⓐ 6%     Ⓒ 12%

Ⓑ 9%     Ⓓ 25%

2. Mr. Petrovich has 11,200 coins in his collection. He plans to add another 1,500 to his collection this year. What is the best estimate of the number of coins Mr. Petrovich will have at the end of this year?

Ⓕ 11,000 coins    Ⓗ 13,000 coins

Ⓖ 12,000 coins    Ⓙ 14,000 coins

3. Ellen enjoys exercise. It usually takes her 9 minutes to jog a mile. What is a reasonable estimate of the time it would take Ellen to jog 5 miles?

Ⓐ less than 30 minutes

Ⓑ between 30 and 40 minutes

Ⓒ between 40 and 50 minutes

Ⓓ more than 50 minutes

4. On Liz's vacation she planned to travel $297\frac{3}{4}$ kilometers on a train. If the train had traveled $74\frac{1}{2}$ kilometers, what is the best estimate of the number of kilometers she had left to travel?

Ⓕ $120\frac{1}{4}$ kilometers

Ⓖ 225 kilometers

Ⓗ 270 kilometers

Ⓙ 370 kilometers

5. This chart shows some of the rivers in Africa.

| River | Length |
|---|---|
| Nile River | 4,145 miles |
| Limpopo River | 1,100 miles |
| Niger River | 2,600 miles |
| Orange River | 1,300 miles |
| Zambezi River | 1,650 miles |

About how much shorter is the Orange River than the Nile River?

_____

**STOP**

    Core Skills Test Prep, Grade 7    Unit 5

# USING COMPUTATION

**Directions:** Darken the circle for the correct answer. Darken the circle for *NH, Not Here*, if the correct answer is not given.

| Try This | Check the answer to a division problem by multiplying. Multiply your answer by the divisor in the problem. That answer should equal the larger number in the problem. |
|---|---|

**Sample A**

$1.5\overline{)45}$

- (A) 3
- (B) 300
- (C) 30
- (D) 0.3
- (E) NH

| Think It Through | The correct answer is C, 30. First, move the decimal in 1.5 to 15. Next, move the decimal one place in 45 to 450, and write the decimal in the quotient. Then, divide as with whole numbers. Last, check the answer by multiplying 30 by 1.5. |
|---|---|

**STOP**

1. $10\frac{1}{4} - 2\frac{3}{4} =$
- (A) $8\frac{1}{2}$
- (B) $8\frac{3}{4}$
- (C) 7
- (D) 13
- (E) NH

2. $43\overline{)8285}$
- (F) 190
- (G) $192\frac{29}{43}$
- (H) $191\frac{42}{43}$
- (J) $192\frac{12}{43}$
- (K) NH

3. $852 \times 29$
- (A) 24,708
- (B) 24,372
- (C) 24,608
- (D) 14,708
- (E) NH

4. $0.7\overline{)0.56}$
- (A) 0.8
- (G) 8
- (H) 80
- (J) 0.08
- (K) NH

5. $3.84 \times 4.6 =$
- (A) 3.840
- (B) 17.664
- (C) 176.64
- (D) 27.664
- (E) NH

6. $\frac{1}{5} \div \frac{1}{8} =$
- (F) $\frac{1}{40}$
- (G) $1\frac{3}{8}$
- (H) $\frac{3}{5}$
- (J) $1\frac{3}{5}$
- (K) NH

**STOP**

# USING COMPUTATION IN CONTEXT

**Directions:** Darken the circle for the correct answer. Darken the circle for NH, Not Here, if the correct answer is not given.

| | |
|---|---|
| **Try This** | Read the word problem carefully. Then set up the word problem as a computation problem. Solve the problem and compare it to the answer choices. |

**Sample A**

Pat's rope measured 54 feet long, and Nick's rope was 65 feet long. What is the total length of the ropes?

Ⓐ 100 feet
Ⓑ 109 feet
Ⓒ 119 feet
Ⓓ 11 feet

| | |
|---|---|
| **Think It Through** | The correct answer is C, 119 feet. To find the combined length of the two ropes, add 54 feet and 65 feet to get 119 feet. |

1. Mrs. Schultz's car has a gas tank that holds 121/2 gallons of gas. She used $\frac{1}{5}$ of a tank of gas. How many gallons did she use?

Ⓐ $2\frac{1}{2}$ gallons
Ⓑ $3\frac{1}{2}$ gallons
Ⓒ 4 gallons
Ⓓ $3\frac{3}{4}$ gallons
Ⓔ NH

2. Gwen was planting tomato plants in a row 6 yards long. She put the plants  yard apart. How many plants were in the row?

Ⓕ $8\frac{2}{3}$
Ⓖ 9
Ⓗ 10
Ⓙ $7\frac{1}{3}$
Ⓚ NH

3. Alex spent $2.40 for cough medicine, $1.29 for cough drops, and $0.79 for tissues. What was the total cost of these items?

Ⓐ $3.88
Ⓑ $3.47
Ⓒ $4.48
Ⓓ $5.48
Ⓔ NH

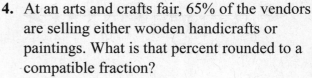

4. At an arts and crafts fair, 65% of the vendors are selling either wooden handicrafts or paintings. What is that percent rounded to a compatible fraction?

Ⓕ $\frac{1}{3}$
Ⓖ $\frac{1}{2}$
Ⓗ $\frac{2}{3}$
Ⓙ $\frac{3}{4}$
Ⓚ NH

**71**

# TEST 1: MATH PROBLEM SOLVING

**Sample A**

Which fraction is greatest in value?

$\frac{2}{12}$     $\frac{2}{4}$     $\frac{2}{2}$     $\frac{2}{6}$

Ⓐ $\frac{2}{12}$       Ⓒ $\frac{2}{2}$

Ⓑ $\frac{2}{4}$       Ⓓ $\frac{2}{6}$

🛑 STOP

**For questions 1–38, darken the circle for the correct answer, or write in the answer.**

1. The stock number on an item is 54.763. What is the value of the 3 in 54.763?

   Ⓐ 3 ten-thousandths

   Ⓑ 3 thousandths

   Ⓒ 3 hundredths

   Ⓓ 3 tenths

2. Light travels at a speed of 186,282 miles per second. How could this number be expressed in scientific notation?

   Ⓕ $1,862.82 \times 10^3$    Ⓗ $1.86282 \times 10^4$

   Ⓖ $1.86282 \times 10^5$    Ⓙ $186.282 \times 10^{-3}$

3. What is the value of point B on the number line?

   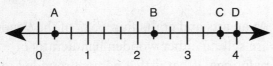

   Ⓐ $2\frac{1}{3}$       Ⓒ $3\frac{2}{3}$

   Ⓑ $\frac{1}{3}$       Ⓓ 4

4. Which fraction does *not* have the same value as the other fractions?

   $6\frac{2}{3}$    $\frac{20}{3}$    $6\frac{9}{12}$    $6\frac{4}{6}$

   Ⓕ $6\frac{2}{3}$       Ⓗ $6\frac{9}{12}$

   Ⓖ $\frac{20}{3}$       Ⓙ $6\frac{4}{6}$

5. Which problem could be solved by the equation $x = 0.3 \times 200$?

   Ⓐ Three hamburgers cost $2. How much does one cost?

   Ⓑ A theater holds 200 people. How many people would be able to attend 3 showings of a movie?

   Ⓒ The regular fare of $200 for a plane ticket was just reduced by 30%. What would the savings be?

   Ⓓ The temperature in an oven was 200 degrees. It was then increased by 0.3 degrees. What is the current oven temperature?

6. Which decimal shows the part of this figure that is shaded?

   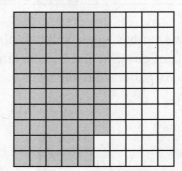

   Ⓕ 5.8       Ⓗ 0.058

   Ⓖ 0.58       Ⓙ 5.08

7. In what way are the numbers in the oval related?

   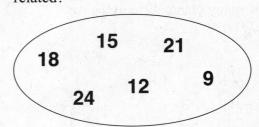

   _____

   _____

➤ GO ON

**72**

8. If $32 = 5d + 7$, what is the value of $d$?

   Ⓐ 2

   Ⓑ 4

   Ⓒ 5

   Ⓓ 8

9. Andy has the 2 cubes shown here. They have the numbers 1, 2, 3, 4, 5, and 6 on their faces. If he rolls the cubes together, what is the probability that the 2 numbers showing at the top of the cubes will total 6 when added together?

   Ⓕ $\frac{1}{4}$

   Ⓖ $\frac{5}{24}$

   Ⓗ $\frac{1}{6}$

   Ⓙ $\frac{5}{36}$

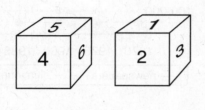

10. Ray uses 4 boards to build 1 step, 10 boards to build 2 steps, and 18 boards to build 3 steps. Following this pattern, how many boards would you expect Ray to use to build 5 steps?

_____

_____

_____

_____

11. At a recent marshmallow-eating contest, the winner ate 20 marshmallows in 5 minutes. At that rate, how many marshmallows would the winner eat if the contest lasted 25 minutes?

   Ⓐ 120

   Ⓑ 100

   Ⓒ 40

   Ⓓ 25

12. Emma bought 2 pairs of socks for $2.95 each. She bought a pair of shoes that cost 8 times as much as a pair of socks. Which expression could be used to determine the cost of the shoes?

   Ⓕ $(8 - 2) + \$2.95$

   Ⓖ $(\$2.95 \times 2) + (\$2.95 \times 8)$

   Ⓗ $(8 + 2) - \$2.95$

   Ⓙ $\$2.95 \times 8$

13. The average (mean) temperature for 4 days was 74 degrees. Which set of temperatures could reasonably show the exact temperatures for the 4 days?

   Ⓐ 74°, 75°, 76°, 77°

   Ⓑ 74°, 72°, 72°, 70°

   Ⓒ 78°, 75°, 74°, 74°

   Ⓓ 72°, 76°, 68°, 80°

14. The camera club is responsible for decorating one of the bulletin boards at school. They change the bulletin board every month. They have three colors of border trim, 5 background colors, and 2 styles of lettering to choose from. If they use 1 border, 1 background color, and 1 style of lettering at a time, how many months of bulletin-board combinations can they make?

   Ⓕ 30 months

   Ⓖ 15 months

   Ⓗ 10 months

   Ⓙ 6 months

© Houghton Mifflin Harcourt Publishing Company

**This table shows the prices of four different kinds of markers. Study the table. Then answer questions 15–17.**

| Markers | | |
|---|---|---|
| **Kind** | **Number in box** | **Price per box** |
| Wide tip | 6 | $3.00 |
| Narrow tip | 10 | $3.50 |
| Pastel colors | 7 | $5.50 |
| Neon colors | 5 | $5.75 |
| Washable | 12 | $5.40 |

15. Becky spent $9.25 for markers. Which two kinds of markers did she buy?

Ⓐ  wide tip and washable

Ⓑ  pastel colors and wide tip

Ⓒ  neon colors and narrow tip

Ⓓ  washable and pastel colors

16. How many more washable markers are in a box than pastel colors?

Ⓕ  5

Ⓖ  6

Ⓗ  7

Ⓙ  19

17. Juan bought a box of markers for which the cost of one marker was the lowest priced of the five kinds. Which kind of marker did he buy?

_____

_____

_____

_____

_____

_____

**Study the following graph. Then answer questions 18–20.**

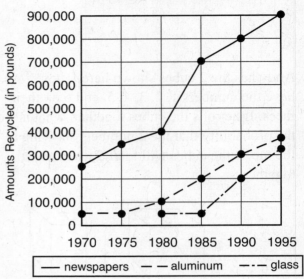

18. In what year did the people of Center City begin to recycle glass?

Ⓐ  1970                Ⓒ  1985

Ⓑ  1980                Ⓓ  1990

19. In what year did the people of Center City recycle four times as much newspaper as glass?

Ⓕ  1975                Ⓗ  1985

Ⓖ  1980                Ⓙ  1990

20. Which of the following conclusions can be made about Center City?

Ⓐ  Recycling is declining in Center City.

Ⓑ  Center City residents need to build a new park.

Ⓒ  Recycling has become important to the residents of Center City.

Ⓓ  Center City residents will probably stop recycling newspapers.

> GO ON

**74**

**21.** Which edge of the cube shown here is parallel to edge CD?

(F) $\overline{CG}$

(G) $\overline{AE}$

(H) $\overline{EF}$

(J) $\overline{BD}$

**22.** Wendy wanted to sew a new tablecloth for her round table. The radius of the table is 18 inches. What is the approximate circumference of the table?
(Use C = $\pi d$ and $\pi$ = 3.14. )

(A) about 113 inches

(B) about 92 inches

(C) about 72 inches

(D) about 57 inches

**23.** There are 4 red beads, 8 yellow beads, and 2 pink beads in a bag. If one bead is picked at random from the bag, what is the probability that it will be red?

(F) $\frac{1}{2}$

(G) $\frac{2}{5}$

(H) $\frac{2}{7}$

(J) $\frac{1}{4}$

**24.** The diameter of this circle is represented by which line segment?

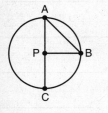

_____

_____

_____

_____

_____

**25.** Which ordered pair in the park represents the location of the jungle gym?

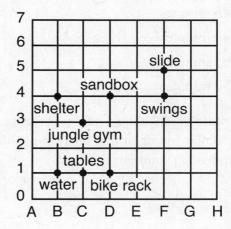

(A) (C, 2)

(B) (D, 3)

(C) (B, 4)

(D) (C, 3)

**26.** Which transformation moves the figure from position A to position B?

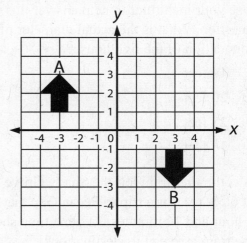

(F) reflection

(G) rotation

(H) translation

(J) extension

**GO ON**

27. Joan's piano lesson begins at 3:35. It ends at 4:05. How many minutes long is the lesson?

   (A) 45 minutes

   (B) 40 minutes

   (C) 35 minutes

   (D) 30 minutes

28. The scale model shown here represents the circular foundation of an 18th-century lighthouse in southern England.

**Scale: 1 inch represents 16 feet**

Use your inch ruler to help answer this question. What is the actual diameter of the foundation of the lighthouse?

   (F) 14 feet

   (G) 20 feet

   (H) 28 feet

   (J) 36 feet

29. A commuter train left the Shady Grove depot at 6:53 A.M. for a trip to Pecan Gap that takes 1 hour and 16 minutes. At what time should the train arrive at its destination?

   _____

   _____

   _____

   _____

30. Juanita competes in races 4 times a year. It takes her between 30 and 35 minutes to run a $4\frac{1}{2}$-mile race. What would be a reasonable time for her to run a $2\frac{1}{4}$-mile race?

   (A) between $6\frac{3}{4}$ and 9 minutes

   (B) between 8 and 10 minutes

   (C) between 15 and 20 minutes

   (D) between 50 and 60 minutes

31. Swimming lessons at the local park district swimming pool cost $18.00 for 2 weeks of lessons. What is the best estimate of the total cost for 7 people to take swimming lessons at the pool?

   (F) $30

   (G) $70

   (H) $90

   (J) $140

32. Drew was leveling a table. One corner had to be raised $\frac{3}{4}$ inch. He had some pieces of wood $\frac{1}{16}$ inch thick. How many pieces of wood would he need to use for the corner to make the table level?

   _____

   _____

   _____

   _____

   _____

   _____

**GO ON**

**76**

**33.** The temperature outside rose 41 degrees during a 12-hour period. If the temperature rose the same number of degrees every hour, what is a good estimate of the number of degrees the temperature rose each hour?

Ⓐ  2 degrees

Ⓑ  3 degrees

Ⓒ  6 degrees

Ⓓ  7 degrees

**34.** About how far is it from Belton to Trell on the map shown here?

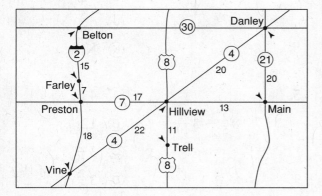

_____ miles

**35.** How many cubes are in this stack?

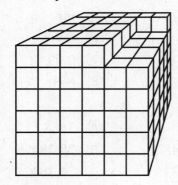

Ⓕ  30

Ⓖ  160

Ⓗ  172

Ⓙ  196

**36.** There are 24 parking spaces in each row in a parking lot. What information is needed to find the maximum number of parking spaces in the parking lot?

Ⓐ  the number of cars parked in each row

Ⓑ  the area of the parking lot

Ⓒ  the number of parking rows

Ⓓ  the number of empty parking spaces

**37.** Each square-shaped box in the pattern shown here decreases in length and width by $\frac{1}{2}$ unit each time. If Box 1 originally measured 12 by 12 units, what would be the dimensions of Box 9?

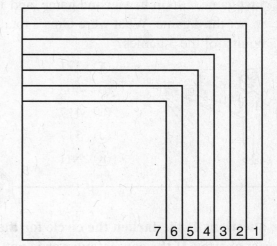

Ⓕ  1 by 1 unit

Ⓖ  4 by 4 units

Ⓗ  5 by 5 units

Ⓙ  8 by 8 units

**38.** Brand A laundry detergent costs more than Brand D. Brand D costs less than Brand X. Brand Z costs more than Brand A. Which of the following is most likely true?

Ⓐ  Brand Z costs more than Brand D.

Ⓑ  Brand X and Brand A cost the same.

Ⓒ  Brand Z costs less than Brand X.

Ⓓ  Brand A costs more than Brand X.

# TEST 2: MATH PROCEDURES

**Sample A**

$$\frac{2}{3} \div \frac{5}{6} =$$

- (A) $\frac{2}{3}$
- (B) $\frac{1}{3}$
- (C) $1\frac{1}{4}$
- (D) $\frac{2}{5}$
- (E) NH

**STOP**

**Sample B**

At the bowling alley Gina scored 133 in her first game, 146 in her second game, and 138 in her third game. What were Gina's total points for the 3 games?

- (F) 371
- (G) 408
- (H) 417
- (J) 517
- (K) NH

**STOP**

**For questions 1–14, darken the circle for the correct answer. If the correct answer is not given, darken the circle for *NH, Not Here*. If no choices are given, write in the answer.**

**1.**

$$8.4 \times 0.934 =$$

- (A) 78.456
- (B) 7.8456
- (C) 0.78456
- (D) 784.56
- (E) NH

**2.**

$$44\overline{)8085}$$

- (F) $183\frac{3}{4}$
- (G) $183\frac{23}{44}$
- (H) $182\frac{33}{44}$
- (J) 183
- (K) NH

**3.**

$$6.183 \times 2.4 =$$

- (A) 14.8392
- (B) 1.48392
- (C) 0.148392
- (D) 148.392
- (E) NH

**4.**

$$2\frac{1}{3} + 4\frac{5}{12}$$

- (F) $6\frac{2}{5}$
- (G) $6\frac{1}{2}$
- (H) $6\frac{3}{4}$
- (J) $6\frac{5}{6}$
- (K) NH

**5.**

$$8\frac{2}{5} - 3\frac{7}{10} =$$

- (A) $4\frac{7}{10}$
- (B) $12\frac{1}{20}$
- (C) $3\frac{7}{10}$
- (D) $3\frac{2}{5}$
- (E) NH

**6.**

$$0.8\overline{)0.72}$$

- (F) 9
- (G) 90
- (H) 0.9
- (J) 0.09
- (K) NH

**7.**

$$\begin{array}{r} 648 \\ \times\ 33 \\ \hline \end{array}$$

- (A) 3888
- (B) 20,384
- (C) 21,384
- (D) 21,284
- (E) NH

**8.**

$$\begin{array}{r} 706 \\ \times\ 285 \\ \hline \end{array}$$

**GO ON**

Unit 5
Core Skills Test Prep, Grade 7

9. Julius and his family drove to New Orleans. On the way there, they drove 298 miles. They took a shorter route back and drove 286 miles. How many miles did they drive altogether?

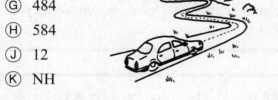

Ⓕ 384

Ⓖ 484

Ⓗ 584

Ⓙ 12

Ⓚ NH

10. The tallest seventh-grade boy is $70\frac{3}{8}$ inches tall. What is his height rounded to the nearest half inch?

Ⓐ 70 inches

Ⓑ 71 inches

Ⓒ $70\frac{1}{2}$ inches

Ⓓ 80 inches

Ⓔ NH

11. Last month, Juanita ran the 100-meter dash in 12.56 seconds. Yesterday, she ran the 100-meter dash in 11.97 seconds. By how much did her time improve from last month?

Ⓕ 0.59 seconds

Ⓖ 0.65 seconds

Ⓗ 0.69 seconds

Ⓙ 0.75 seconds

Ⓚ NH

12. Lauren read 3 books last weekend. She made this table to show the time she spent reading.

| Lauren's Weekend Reading | | | |
|---|---|---|---|
| Books | 1 | 2 | 3 |
| Hours | $4\frac{3}{4}$ | $3\frac{3}{4}$ | $1\frac{1}{4}$ |

How many hours did Lauren spend reading the 3 books?

Ⓐ $8\frac{3}{4}$ hours

Ⓑ $8\frac{1}{4}$ hours

Ⓒ $7\frac{1}{4}$ hours

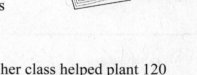

Ⓓ $9\frac{1}{2}$ hours

Ⓔ NH

13. Tamiko and her class helped plant 120 saplings at local parks on Earth Day. If 30 of the saplings were maple trees, what percent of the trees were maple trees?

Ⓕ 90%

Ⓖ 75%

Ⓗ 25%

Ⓙ $33\frac{1}{3}$%

Ⓚ NH

14. Molly bought 6 pounds of cornmeal at 39¢ per pound. How much did she spend on the cornmeal?

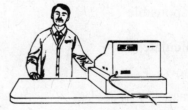

_____

_____

_____

**STOP**

**79**

# Unit 7: Listening

## UNDERSTANDING WORD MEANINGS

**Directions: Darken the circle for the word or words that best complete the sentence you hear.**

| **Try This** | Listen carefully to the sentence. Then look at the answer choices. Decide which words you know are wrong. Then look at the remaining words to make your choice. |
| --- | --- |

**Sample A**

   (A) fur      (C) teeth

   (B) eyes     (D) bones

| **Think It Through** | The correct answer is C, Fangs are a kind of "teeth." |
| --- | --- |

**STOP**

1. (A) confuse
   (B) miss
   (C) determine
   (D) report

2. (F) usual
   (G) unimportant
   (H) worthwhile
   (J) serious

3. (A) closed
   (B) unreliable
   (C) blameless
   (D) responsible

4. (F) calculate
   (G) know
   (H) grasp
   (J) estimate

5. (A) ratify
   (B) uphold
   (C) support
   (D) cancel

6. (F) lingering
   (G) hurrying
   (H) overtaking
   (J) running

7. (A) not serious
   (B) silly
   (C) not planned
   (D) deliberate

8. (F) vase
   (G) box
   (H) wreath
   (J) handful

9. (A) gather    (C) retain
   (B) collect   (D) distribute

**Write your answer to the following question:**

10. _____

_____

**STOP**

# BUILDING LISTENING SKILLS

**Directions: Darken the circle for the word or words that best answer the question.**

| **Try This** | Form a picture of the passage in your mind. Listen carefully for details given in the passage. |
|---|---|

**Sample A**

Ⓐ snow

Ⓑ rain

Ⓒ cold

Ⓓ heat

| **Think It Through** | The correct answer is A. The paragraph says that people in cold climates build houses with sloping roofs so the <u>snow</u> will slide off easily. |
|---|---|

🛑 STOP

---

1. Ⓐ clothing   Ⓒ paper
   Ⓑ tents   Ⓓ blankets

2. Ⓕ cattle   Ⓗ chickens
   Ⓖ sheep   Ⓙ goats

3. Ⓐ the Pacific Northwest
   Ⓑ the Southeast
   Ⓒ the Northeast
   Ⓓ the Southwest

4. Ⓕ they burned
   Ⓖ a hurricane
   Ⓗ an earthquake
   Ⓙ a tornado

5. Ⓐ on September 4
   Ⓑ on September 22
   Ⓒ in October
   Ⓓ on September 15

6. Ⓕ individual classrooms
   Ⓖ Jackson Junior High School
   Ⓗ the school gym
   Ⓙ the principal's office

7. Ⓐ the drive will not be successful
   Ⓑ the principal may not approve the school-supply drive
   Ⓒ the students will volunteer to adopt another school
   Ⓓ Jackson Junior High School will rebuild and reopen soon

8. Ⓕ in a science book
   Ⓖ in a teen magazine
   Ⓗ in a newspaper
   Ⓙ in a news magazine

9. Ⓐ make the goal specific
   Ⓑ have as much time as possible
   Ⓒ work on several goals at a time
   Ⓓ try to achieve the goal without help

10. Ⓕ the time available to reach the goal
    Ⓖ their interests, strengths, and values
    Ⓗ who can help with achieving the goal
    Ⓙ the reward for achieving the goal

🛑 STOP

# TEST

**Sample A**

   Ⓐ reluctant    Ⓒ friendly

   Ⓑ cold       Ⓓ small

---

**For questions 1–12, darken the circle for the word or words that best complete the sentence you hear.**

1.  Ⓐ energetic
     Ⓑ slow
     Ⓒ precise
     Ⓓ jerky

2.  Ⓕ cry
     Ⓖ yelp
     Ⓗ squirm
     Ⓙ suffer

3.  Ⓐ harsh
     Ⓑ kind
     Ⓒ foolish
     Ⓓ clever

4.  Ⓕ bring in
     Ⓖ send away
     Ⓗ accept
     Ⓙ return

5.  Ⓐ gray
     Ⓑ calm
     Ⓒ silent
     Ⓓ stormy

6.  Ⓕ scarce    Ⓗ meager
     Ⓖ large     Ⓙ small

7.  Ⓐ wandering
     Ⓑ settled
     Ⓒ stationary
     Ⓓ resident

8.  Ⓕ involved
     Ⓖ biased
     Ⓗ uninvolved
     Ⓙ subjective

9.  Ⓐ worthwhile
     Ⓑ useless
     Ⓒ pointless
     Ⓓ unprofitable

10.  Ⓕ bitter
      Ⓖ tasteless
      Ⓗ bland
      Ⓙ delicious

11.  Ⓐ desire
      Ⓑ skill
      Ⓒ inability
      Ⓓ job

12.  Ⓕ noticeable
      Ⓖ invisible
      Ⓗ insignificant
      Ⓙ subtle

**Write your answer to the following question:**

13. _____

     _____

     _____

**GO ON**

                  Unit 7
Core Skills Test Prep, Grade 7

**Sample B**

- (A) hobby magazine
- (B) history book
- (C) science magazine
- (D) psychology book

**STOP**

For questions 14–26, listen to the passage. Then darken the circle for the word or words that best answer the question, or write in the answer.

14. (A) should exercise more
    (B) should take vitamin pills
    (C) need to learn about nutrition
    (D) buy more vitamins than other people

15. (F) "A Good Diet"
    (G) "Everyone Needs Vitamins"
    (H) "Why Take Vitamin Supplements?"
    (J) "Foods to Avoid"

16. (A) to inform
    (B) to persuade
    (C) to entertain
    (D) to inspire

17. (F) 1962
    (G) 1964
    (H) 1975
    (J) 1984

18. (A) set a new speed record
    (B) wrote newspaper articles
    (C) flew missions during World War II
    (D) flew missions during the Korean War

19. (F) put an American into space
    (G) help Glenn become a hero
    (H) train test pilots
    (J) win the Korean War

20. (A) an astronaut
    (B) a newspaper reporter
    (C) a test pilot
    (D) a Marine Corps pilot

21. (F) a squirrel
    (G) a dog
    (H) one of the friends
    (J) the writer's little brother

22. (A) to please their parents
    (B) to make money
    (C) to help their neighbors
    (D) to complete a school project

23. (F) mowing lawns
    (G) taking care of children
    (H) walking a dog
    (J) delivering newspapers

24. (A) Biff ran and pulled Alex with him.
    (B) Alex did not want people to see them.
    (C) They took pictures of Alex and Biff.
    (D) Biff was very shy.

25. (F) Janet's
    (G) Luis's
    (H) Joey's
    (J) Alex's

26. _____

_____

**STOP**

# Unit 8: Language

## PREWRITING, COMPOSING, AND EDITING

**Directions: Read each sentence carefully. Then darken the circle for the correct answer to each question.**

| **Try This** | Pretend that you are writing each sentence. Use the rules you have learned for capitalization, punctuation, word usage, and sentence structure to choose the correct answer. |
|---|---|

### A Vacation on a Working Ranch

Celina and her family want to spend their vacation at a working ranch. Celina is trying to find more information about working ranches. She decides to write a letter to one of the ranches.

**Sample A**

> Dear Director,
>
> I am writing to ask you to send me information about vacationing at your working ranch. My family and I such a vacation. Please send the information as soon as possible. We are anxious to plan our vacation.

Which of these is *not* a complete sentence?

Ⓐ I am writing to ask you to send me information about vacationing at your working ranch.

Ⓑ My family and I such a vacation.

Ⓒ Please send the information as soon as possible.

Ⓓ We are anxious to plan our vacation.

| **Think It Through** | The correct answer is B. My family and I such a vacation is not a complete sentence. |
|---|---|

### Writing a Research Paper

Ken is studying coral reefs in geography class. He is interested in learning more about the Great Barrier Reef along the northeast coast of Australia. Ken decides to use the Great Barrier Reef as the subject of his research paper for geography class.

1. Once Ken decides what to include in his research paper, what can he do to organize his paper?

Ⓐ plan a trip to the Great Barrier Reef

Ⓑ ask people what they know about coral reefs

Ⓒ make an outline or web of the information to include in the paper

Ⓓ determine the length of the paper

Ken found books in the library on the Great Barrier Reef. Use the Table of Contents and Index from the books to answer questions 2–6.

## Book 1

### Table of Contents

## Book 2

### Index

2. Ken can find information in Chapter 1 of Book 1 about all of the following except —

   (F) Australia

   (G) cyclones

   (H) colors of corals

   (J) breakwater

3. Which pages in Book 2 would help Ken learn about Captain Cook's discovery of Australia?

   (A) 13–17

   (B) 48–49

   (C) 57–61

   (D) 21, 24

4. Which pages in Book 2 would have information about the types of coral found in the Great Barrier Reef?

   (F) 1–6

   (G) 21, 22

   (H) 25

   (J) 57–61

5. On which pages in Book 2 would Ken find information about caves found in the Great Barrier Reef?

   (A) 18, 23, 35

   (B) 21, 22

   (C) 9, 11, 12

   (D) 58–60

**Write your answer for the following question:**

6. Which chapter in Book 1 would have information about the kinds of fish that inhabit the Great Barrier Reef?

   _____

   _____

   _____

   _____

   _____

▶ GO ON

Name _____  Date _____

**Here is a rough draft of the first part of Ken's paper. Read the rough draft carefully. Then answer questions 7–12.**

## The Great Barrier Reef

The Great Barrier Reef forms the largest reef on earth. It is 1,250
**(1)**                                                      **(2)**
miles long and is made up of the hardened skeletons of millions of dead

water animals called coral polyps. The Great Barrier Reef located in
**(3)**
the South Pacific Ocean. It lies along the northeast coast of Australia.
**(4)**
The reef contains a system of deep channels, lagoons, shallow pools,
**(5)**
underwater caves, and ledges. The Great Barrier Reef forms a
**(6)**
breakwater, or wall, against the ocean. The reef is constantly battered
**(7)**
by ocean waves.

Billions of living coral polyps make their home on the reef. Some of
**(8)**                                                              **(9)**
these sea creatures are as big as a dime others are as tiny as a pinhead.

Their brilliant colors include green, yellow, blue, red, and purple. Coral
**(10)**                                                            **(11)**
takes calcium from the ocean, changes it into lime, and uses the lime to

construct its home on top of the dead coral. I was impressed with the
**(12)**
quality and taste of the fish. In this home the coral remains for life.
**(13)**
In 1770, Captain James Cook was the first person to lead an
**(14)**
expedition to explore the Great Barrier Reef. He was the captain of the
**(15)**
ship *Endeavor*; and, perhaps, he was its navigator. This flat-bottomed
**(16)**
wooden ship was 106 feet long and 29 feet wide. Cook and his crew
**(17)**
explored the coast of Australia.

**GO ON**

Unit 8
Core Skills Test Prep, Grade 7

**7.** Which group of words is *not* a complete sentence?

(F) 1

(G) 2

(H) 3

(J) 4

**8.** Which is the topic sentence of the second paragraph?

(A) 8

(B) 9

(C) 10

(D) 11

**9.** Which sentence could be added after sentence 7?

(F) Captain James Cook explored many islands in the Pacific Ocean.

(G) The reef is sturdy, however, providing a home to thousands of sea creatures.

(H) Barracuda can be seen hunting herring in the lagoons.

(J) The colorful coral is harvested for jewelry.

**10.** Which sentence does *not* belong in Ken's paper?

(A) 9

(B) 10

(C) 11

(D) 12

**11.** In sentence 15, the word *perhaps* does not appropriately connect the ideas. Which word or words should be used instead?

(F) however

(G) then

(H) thirdly

(J) in addition

**12.** Rewrite sentence 13 making the idea clearer.

_____

_____

_____

_____

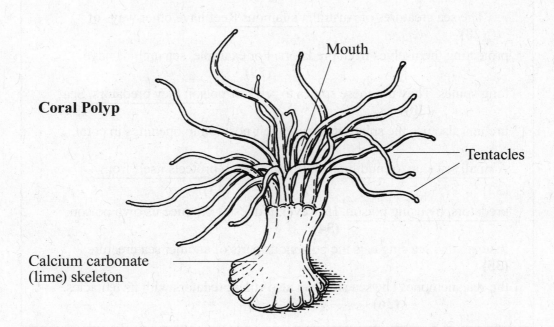

**Coral Polyp**

Mouth

Tentacles

Calcium carbonate (lime) skeleton

Core Skills Test Prep, Grade 7

Name _____  Date _____

**Here is the next part of Ken's rough draft for his paper. This part has certain words and phrases underlined. Read the draft carefully. Then answer questions 13–20.**

<u>Life is dangerous</u> for the sea creatures of the Great Barrier Reef.
(18)

Most need protection from predators, or creatures that kill other
(19)

animals for food. Many animals are able to <u>survived</u> because their
(20)

colors or patterns camouflage them. For example, some brightly colored
(21)

fish live among the brightly colored corals and blend in with their

surroundings. Other fish change colors to match their surroundings.
(22)

Octopi are able to change their colors instantly. <u>She can change</u> quickly
(23)                                                                        (24)

from brown to blue to white to green to red to purple to stripes!

<u>Lagoons, shallow ponds with no place to hide are dangerous places</u>
(25)

<u>for colorful fish.</u> The bright colors of these fish would make it easy for
(26)

predators to see them. Therefore, fish that live in lagoons have dull
(27)

colors for protection.

The sea creatures of <u>Australia's famous Reef</u> have other ways of
(28)

protecting themselves from predators. For example, sea urchins have
(29)

long spines. They use these spines to prick or <u>poison they predators.</u> Sea
(30)                                                                        (31)

urchins also use the spines to secure their position in openings in coral.

A <u>small sea slug, or nudibranch</u> has no shell. <u>It protects itself from</u>
(32)                                                    (33)

<u>predators, by using poison.</u> However, it doesn't produce its own poison.
(34)

Instead, this sea slug eats the poisonous parts of another sea creature,
(35)

the sea anemone. The sea slug can also sting predators with its tentacles.
(36)

▶ **GO ON**

Unit 8
Core Skills Test Prep, Grade 7

**13.** In sentence 18, <u>Life is dangerous</u> is best written —

  Ⓐ Life was dangerous

  Ⓑ Life are dangerous

  Ⓒ Life were dangerous

  Ⓓ As it is written.

**14.** In sentence 20, <u>survived</u> is best written —

  Ⓕ has survived

  Ⓖ survive

  Ⓗ have survived

  Ⓙ As it is written.

**15.** In sentence 24, <u>She can change</u> is best written —

  Ⓐ They can change

  Ⓑ He can change

  Ⓒ We can change

  Ⓓ As it is written.

**16.** Correctly rewrite sentence 25, <u>Lagoons, shallow ponds with no place to hide are dangerous places for colorful fish.</u>

_____

_____

_____

_____

**17.** In sentence 28, <u>Australia's famous Reef</u> is best written —

  Ⓕ australia's famous reef

  Ⓖ Australia's famous reef

  Ⓗ Australia's Famous Reef

  Ⓙ As it is written.

**18.** In sentence 30, <u>poison they predators</u> is best written —

  Ⓐ poison our predators

  Ⓑ poison his predators

  Ⓒ poison their predators

  Ⓓ As it is written.

**19.** In sentence 32, <u>small sea slug, or nudibranch</u> is best written —

  Ⓕ small sea slug or nudibranch

  Ⓖ small, sea, slug or nudibranch

  Ⓗ small sea slug, or nudibranch,

  Ⓙ As it is written.

**20.** Correctly rewrite sentence 33, <u>It protects itself from predators, by using poison.</u>

_____

_____

_____

_____

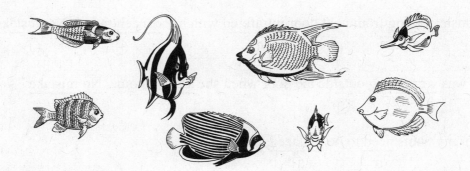

STOP

# IDENTIFYING MISSPELLED WORDS

**Directions: Read each sentence carefully. If one of the words is misspelled, darken the circle for that word. If all the words are spelled correctly, darken the circle for *No mistake*.**

| **Try This** | Read each sentence carefully. If you are not sure of an answer, first decide which answer choices are spelled correctly. Then see if you can recognize the misspelled word from your reading experience. |
| --- | --- |

**Sample A**

We were <u>planning</u> to get <u>something</u> to eat at <u>intramission</u>. <u>No mistake</u>
       Ⓐ          Ⓑ         Ⓒ     Ⓓ

| **Think It Through** | The correct answer is C. The prefix should be <u>inter</u>–, not *intra*–. The correct spelling is i-n-t-e-r-m-i-s-s-i-o-n. |
| --- | --- |

🛑 STOP

1.  The two groups <u>reached</u> a <u>compromise</u> after a week of <u>discussion</u>. <u>No mistake</u>
            Ⓐ      Ⓑ               Ⓒ      Ⓓ

2.  Mr. McDonough will <u>announce</u> his <u>candidatcy</u> at a press <u>conference</u> next Friday. <u>No mistake</u>
                 Ⓕ         Ⓖ             Ⓗ           Ⓙ

3.  We <u>purifyed</u> the water with an <u>iodine</u> <u>tablet</u>. <u>No mistake</u>
   Ⓐ                    Ⓑ  Ⓒ    Ⓓ

4.  Toshi's quick <u>reaction</u> <u>avertted</u> a potential <u>accident</u>. <u>No mistake</u>
             Ⓕ     Ⓖ           Ⓗ     Ⓙ

5.  I am <u>doutful</u> that we will <u>arrive</u> in time for <u>dinner</u>. <u>No mistake</u>
    Ⓐ             Ⓑ          Ⓒ    Ⓓ

6.  The loud music <u>coming</u> from next door <u>intrafered</u> with my <u>concentration</u>. <u>No mistake</u>
             Ⓕ            Ⓖ        Ⓗ    Ⓙ

7.  The puppy was <u>wimpering</u> <u>outside</u> the door when she <u>arrived</u> home. <u>No mistake</u>
             Ⓐ    Ⓑ               Ⓒ      Ⓓ

8.  The <u>souls</u> of my boots <u>need</u> to be <u>replaced</u>. <u>No mistake</u>
     Ⓕ         Ⓖ     Ⓗ    Ⓙ

🛑 STOP

**90**

Name _____  Date _____

# TEST

## Sample A

The world's first public railroad opened
**(1)**
in England in 1825. It operated between
**(2)**
the towns of Stockton and Darlington, a

distance of 20 miles.

By 1830 railways were operating in
**(3)**
France, Germany, Canada, Spain and,

Switzerland.

How is sentence 3 best written?

Ⓐ By 1830 railways were operating in France and Germany, Canada, Spain and Switzerland.

Ⓑ By 1830 railways were operating in, France, Germany, Canada, Spain, and Switzerland.

Ⓒ By 1830 railways were operating in France, Germany, Canada, Spain, and Switzerland.

Ⓓ As it is written.

**STOP**

---

### The Olympic Games

Carl hopes to attend the next summer Olympic Games. Carl decides to write a letter to the United States Olympic Committee to learn more about the Olympics.

1. Where would Carl find more information about the Olympic Games?

Ⓐ textbook

Ⓑ thesaurus

Ⓒ dictionary

Ⓓ encyclopedia

2. Why is Carl writing a letter to the United States Olympic Committee?

_____

_____

_____

Carl used a dictionary to look up some words he wants to use in his letter to the United States Olympic Committee. Use the dictionary entry and the Pronunciation Guide to answer questions 3 and 4.

> **pen•tath•lon** [pen tath′ lən] n. An athletic contest that features each athlete participating in five different events.

### Pronunciation Guide

at; āpe; fär; câre; end; mē; it; īce; pîerce; hot; ōld; sông; fôrk; oil; out; up; ūse; rüle; pùll; tûrn; chin; sing; shop; thin; this; hw in white; zh in treasure. The symbol ə stands for the unstressed vowel sound in about, taken, pencil, lemon, and circus.

3. What is the correct way to divide <u>pentathlon</u> into syllables?

Ⓕ pen ta thlon     Ⓗ pent a thlon

Ⓖ pen tath lon     Ⓙ pent ath lon

4. The "a" in <u>pentathlon</u> sounds most like the vowel sound in —

Ⓐ handkerchief     Ⓑ negative

Ⓒ partnership     Ⓓ everyday

**GO ON**

Unit 8

Core Skills Test Prep, Grade 7

Name _____  Date _____

**Here is a rough draft of the first part of Carl's letter. Read the rough draft carefully. Then answer questions 5 and 6.**

> Dear U.S. Olympic Committee Members,
>
> I am an enthusiastic fan of the Olympic Games! I especially, the
> **(1)**                                                    **(2)**
> events in the Summer Games. I am writing for more information about
> **(3)**
> the Olympics.
>
> I know the Olympic Games consist of the Summer Games and the
> **(4)**
> Winter Games. How is it decided where the games will be held? What
> **(5)**                                                         **(6)**
> events are held in the Summer Games, and what are held in the
>
> Winter Games?
>
> I never miss the opening ceremonies of each Olympic Game. The
> **(7)**                                                       **(8)**
> lighting of the Olympic Flame is awesome! I've read that the lighted
> **(9)**
> torch is brought from the valley of Olympia, Greece, by cross-country
>
> runners. My aunt lived in Greece for a year. What other traditions are
> **(10)**                              **(11)**
> practiced at the opening ceremonies of the Olympic Games?

5. What is the best way to write sentence 2?

   F  I especially, enjoy the events in the Summer Games.

   G  I, especially, enjoy the events in the summer games.

   H  I especially enjoy the events in the Summer Games.

   J  As it is written.

6. Which sentence does *not* belong in this letter? Write the number.

   _____

   _____

   _____

   _____

   _____

Unit 8
Core Skills Test Prep, Grade 7

**Here is the next part of Carl's rough draft for his letter. This part has certain words and phrases underlined. Read the draft carefully. Then answer questions 7–12.**

I have read that an Olympic athlete must be a citizen of the sponsor country.
**(12)**

Does an athlete actually have to live in the country they represent?
**(13)**

Starting with the 1988 Olympics professional athletes were allowed to compete.
**(14)**

National Olympic committees are allowed to pay our athletes while they train
**(15)**

for the Olympics. How much money does the United States Olympic Committee
**(16)**

pay athletes?

In "Modern Olympic Games the fifth chapter of *A History of the Olympics*, I
**(17)**

read that each country is allowed to use its own method for selecting athletes for

the Games. To be chosen from the United States, an athlete must finish high in
**(18)**

the competitions. Will this method of selection ever change?
**(19)**

How are Olympic events judged? I know that in diving, figure skating, and
**(20)**                                **(21)**

gymnastics events, medalists are chosen by judges based on points awarded for

their performances. How are medalists chosen in swimming and track events?
**(22)**

I have one last question. Is it true that the Olympic Games were canceled
**(23)**                        **(24)**

during world Wars I and II?

I look forward to receiving answers to my questions. I appreciate your time
**(25)**                                                **(26)**

and attention.

Sincerely yours,
Carl Hafner

Core Skills Test Prep, Grade 7

**7.** In sentence 13, <u>they represent?</u> is best written —

Ⓐ he or she represents?

Ⓑ you represent?

Ⓒ we represent?

Ⓓ As it is written.

**8.** In sentence 14, <u>Starting with the 1988 Olympics</u> is best written —

Ⓕ Starting with the 1988, Olympics

Ⓖ Starting with the 1988 Olympics,

Ⓗ Starting, with the 1988 Olympics

Ⓙ As it is written.

**9.** What word should be substituted for "our" in sentence 15, <u>pay our athletes?</u>

_____

_____

_____

_____

**10.** Correctly rewrite sentence 17, <u>"Modern Olympic Games the fifth</u> —

Ⓐ "Modern Olympic Games," the fifth

Ⓑ Modern Olympic Games the fifth

Ⓒ "Modern Olympic" Games the fifth

Ⓓ As it is written.

**11.** In sentence 21, <u>in diving, figure skating, and gymnastics</u> is best written —

Ⓕ in diving, figure, skating, and gymnastics

Ⓖ in diving figure skating and gymnastics

Ⓗ in diving, figure skating and, gymnastics

Ⓙ As it is written.

**12.** In sentence 24, <u>world Wars I and II?</u> is best written —

Ⓐ world war one and two?

Ⓑ World war I and II?

Ⓒ World Wars I and II?

Ⓓ As it is written.

**▶ GO ON**

Name _____  Date _____

**For questions 13–24, read each sentence carefully. If one of the words is misspelled, darken the circle for that word. If all the words are spelled correctly, then darken the circle for _No mistake_.**

**13.** Dr. Rivera <u>treats</u> a number of <u>patience</u> at the West Side <u>Clinic</u>. <u>No mistake</u>
      Ⓕ           Ⓖ           Ⓗ   Ⓙ

**14.** The <u>pressure</u> <u>intensifyed</u> as the gymnastics competition moved into the final <u>stages</u>. <u>No mistake</u>
      Ⓐ    Ⓑ                                 Ⓒ    Ⓓ

**15.** The <u>winning</u> rose at the <u>annual</u> garden show has a <u>suttle</u> fragrance. <u>No mistake</u>
      Ⓕ            Ⓖ             Ⓗ        Ⓙ

**16.** The <u>manager</u> gave us <u>complementary</u> tickets to the next <u>matinee</u>. <u>No mistake</u>
      Ⓐ           Ⓑ              Ⓒ    Ⓓ

**17.** Mary <u>canceled</u> her <u>reservation</u> when she <u>herd</u> the news. <u>No mistake</u>
      Ⓕ        Ⓖ        Ⓗ      Ⓙ

**18.** Beautiful <u>frescoes</u> <u>adorned</u> the walls of the <u>ancient</u> temple. <u>No mistake</u>
      Ⓐ    Ⓑ          Ⓒ      Ⓓ

**19.** <u>Literatcy</u> <u>continues</u> to be an important <u>issue</u> in our country. <u>No mistake</u>
      Ⓕ    Ⓖ              Ⓗ        Ⓙ

**20.** The United Nations is a <u>truly</u> <u>intranational</u> <u>organization</u>. <u>No mistake</u>
                   Ⓐ    Ⓑ    Ⓒ    Ⓓ

**21.** The <u>seem</u> on my shirt <u>started</u> to <u>unravel</u>. <u>No mistake</u>
      Ⓕ        Ⓖ   Ⓗ    Ⓙ

**22.** The American team <u>prevailled</u> over the German team in the <u>volleyball</u> <u>match</u>. <u>No mistake</u>
          Ⓐ                        Ⓑ  Ⓒ    Ⓓ

**23.** Reynaldo was a <u>talented</u> <u>amateur</u> tennis <u>player</u>. <u>No mistake</u>
            Ⓕ    Ⓖ      Ⓗ    Ⓙ

**24.** My <u>grandfather</u> liked to sit on the <u>porch</u> swing in the evening and <u>wittle</u>. <u>No mistake</u>
      Ⓐ               Ⓑ          Ⓒ    Ⓓ

**STOP**

# Unit 9: Practice Test 1

## READING COMPREHENSION

 You have 35 minutes to complete this test. Use the answer sheets on page 127 to mark your answers.

**Sample A**     **Cliff Dwellings**

Mesa Verde National Park is located in southwestern Colorado and has some of the most astounding cliff dwellings found in the United States. Approximately eight hundred years ago, the Anasazi people used stone blocks to construct apartment-like dwellings in the caves of the canyon walls.

Which of these is a *fact* stated in the selection?

Ⓐ The cliff dwellings have lasted because they were built well.

Ⓑ The cliff dwellings were never completed.

Ⓒ The Anasazi should have built with brick.

Ⓓ The Anasazi cliff

**For questions 1–33, carefully read each selection and the questions that follow. Darken the circle for the correct answer, or write in your answer.**

### Chicago

Skyscrapers tower
along Lake Michigan
like building blocks.

They seem to lean
toward one another
as if for support.

In their glass sides we see
a reflection in primary colors
of sunset, water, and parks.

Unknowing, they take in
their surroundings and return them
to us as a dream.

1. The poem compares the reflection from the skyscrapers' glass sides to —

Ⓐ real life.

Ⓑ a dream.

Ⓒ a subconscious desire.

Ⓓ an artist's inspiration.

2. This poem was probably written to describe —

Ⓕ how Chicago's skyscrapers look.

Ⓖ how Chicago is not a dream.

Ⓗ a sunset on Lake Michigan.

Ⓙ buildings that look like they are dreaming.

3. The buildings are compared to —

Ⓐ sunsets.

Ⓑ blocks.

Ⓒ parks.

Ⓓ glass.

**GO ON**

## Recycling Plastics

The best way to solve the problem of throw-away plastics is to find practical ways to reuse them. Many useful things are being made from recycled plastics. There are more than fifty types of plastics in use. They are made using a variety of chemicals, dyes, and processes. The different properties of plastics make them suitable for different types of recycled products. The chart below shows the types of plastic products used to recycle into new products. The six codes allow recyclers to separate plastics into groups of types that have the same properties.

## PLASTICS RECYCLING CHART

| Symbol | Uses | Recycled Products (made from recyclable plastics) |
|---|---|---|
| 1 PETE | Plastic soft drink bottles, mouthwash jars, peanut butter and salad dressing bottles | Liquid soap bottles, strapping, fiberfill for winter coats, surfboards, paintbrushes, fuzz on tennis balls, soft drink bottles, film, egg cartons, skis, carpets, boats |
| 2 HDPE | Milk, water, and juice containers; grocery bags; toys; liquid detergent bottles | Soft drink bottle base cups, flowerpots, drain pipes, signs, stadium seats, trash cans, recycling bins, traffic-barrier cones, golf bag liners, detergent bottles, toys |
| 3 V | Clear food packaging, shampoo bottles | Floor mats, pipes, hose, mud flaps |
| 4 LDPE | Bread bags, frozen food bags, grocery bags | Garbage bag liners, grocery bags, multipurpose bags |
| 5 PP | Ketchup bottles, yogurt containers and margarine tubs, medicine bottles | Manhole steps, paint buckets, videocassette storage cases, ice scrapers, fast food trays, lawn mower wheels, automobile battery parts |
| 6 PS | Compact disk jackets, coffee cups, knives, spoons, forks, cafeteria trays, grocery meat trays, fast food sandwich containers | License plate holders, golf course and septic tank drainage systems, desktop accessories, hanging files, food service trays, flower pots, trash cans, videocassettes |

**4.** What is the code symbol for plastic products that can be recycled into hose?

   Ⓕ PP

   Ⓖ V

   Ⓗ HDPE

   Ⓙ PS

**5.** What is the correct code number for such products as bread bags and grocery bags?

   Ⓐ 1

   Ⓑ 3

   Ⓒ 4

   Ⓓ 5

**6.** What is the purpose of the symbols on plastic products?

   Ⓕ to make it easy for recyclers to sort plastics

   Ⓖ to indicate to consumers what new products will be made from the product

   Ⓗ to indicate to scientists the properties of the product

   Ⓙ to indicate to stores how much to charge for the product

**7.** Which of the following shows an original product and its recyclable product?

   Ⓐ peanut butter jars into mud flaps

   Ⓑ detergent bottles into grocery bags

   Ⓒ bread bags into surfboards

   Ⓓ medicine bottles into ice scrapers

**8.** List three recyclable products that can be made from videocassette cases and compact disk jackets.

_____

_____

_____

**9.** If you wanted to learn more about recycling plastics, which of the following articles would you choose to read?

   Ⓕ "Solving the Solid Waste Problem"

   Ⓖ "The History of Durable Goods"

   Ⓗ "Plastic Surgery Success Stories"

   Ⓙ "Manufacturing Plastics"

**10.** If the author added a sentence to the end of the introduction, which of these would best fit?

   Ⓐ Plastic "wood" never rots or splinters or gets termites.

   Ⓑ Then the plastics, grouped by code, can be shipped to companies that recycle plastics.

   Ⓒ Plastics are strong and used for thousands of purposes.

   Ⓓ Too many plastic products are disposed of immediately after using them just once.

**11.** Which code symbol is used for original plastic products that can be turned into recyclable plastic products such as skis, egg cartons, and film?

_____

_____

_____

**GO ON**

**98**

# The Magic Tapestry: A Chinese Folktale

Long ago a widow lived in a cottage with her three sons. She supported the family by weaving tapestries. The tapestries were exquisite works of art that sold for much gold. One day the widow started a new tapestry. She wove into her fabric a magnificent mansion surrounded by brilliant flower gardens. Receding into the distance were rolling hills and towering mountains. Every day for months the widow worked on the tapestry. With *painstaking* care she added intricate details. She created a babbling brook with exotic fish, then wove a graceful footbridge.

Meanwhile Li Mo, her eldest son, and Li Tu, her middle son, began complaining. "When are you going to finish? We have no rice, and our clothes are ragged," Li Mo said. "Hurry and finish so that we can sell the tapestry," Li Tu demanded.

But their mother said nothing. She continued working at the loom from sunrise until late at night. Li Ju, her youngest son, became a woodcutter so that the family could eat.

One day after toiling for more than a year, the widow announced that the tapestry was almost complete. As Li Ju watched, she wove a resemblance of herself into the wall hanging. "This must be your dream," Li Ju said with conviction. The widow wove Li Ju's image into the work.

The other two brothers came in and tried to pry the tapestry off the loom. But their mother wouldn't let them touch it. She said, "This is a picture of everything I wish for and cherish. All my children should be in it, but I haven't had time to weave you in."

"What does it matter? Just give it to us so that we can sell it," Li Mo said. "Yes, all we care about is the gold," Li Tu added cruelly.

Just then a tremendous wind ripped the tapestry from the loom. The treasured work flew out the window and vanished into the eastern sky. The family raced outside but could not *retrieve* it. The widow was devastated. She called Li Mo and told him to travel east in search of the tapestry. "If you don't find it, I will surely die," she said.

Li Mo traveled east for a month; then he came to an old woman who lived in a stone hut. Outside the hut was a stone stallion. The woman told Li Mo that the fairies of Sun Mountain had stolen the tapestry. She said that Li Mo should pierce his finger and bleed on the stone horse. The stallion would take him to Sun Mountain. The old woman described the fiery mountains and icy seas he would have to cross on his journey. Li Mo shuddered at the thought of blood, fire, and ice. But when the old woman offered him a bag of gold, he gladly took it and journeyed to the big city, forgetting about the tapestry.

The widow was becoming weaker. When Li Mo did not return she sent Li Tu. But when Li Tu met the old woman in the hut he also accepted the gold and went to the big city. Li Ju pleaded with his mother to let him search for the tapestry. He knew that his mother was very ill.

When Li Ju reached the stone hut, he eagerly listened to the old woman's instructions. When she offered him a bag of gold, he refused. "I must find the tapestry or my mother will die," he said. Courageously he galloped through the fires and over the icy seas. At last he arrived at Sun Mountain. He was greeted by a beautiful fairy dressed in crimson. The fairy said that she would return the tapestry. The next morning she folded it and handed it to Li Ju. She bid him farewell, and Li Ju journeyed homeward. He hurried because he knew his mother must be near death. Finally he arrived and hung the tapestry on the wall so that his mother could see it. Magically the tapestry expanded until it became a giant landscape. Mother and son walked into the peaceful scene. Waiting for them at the door of the mansion was the fairy dressed in crimson. Li Ju married the fairy, and the three of them lived contentedly on the lovely estate.

One day two beggars who were really Li Mo and Li Tu knocked at the iron gate of the mansion. But a ferocious windstorm carried them away and deposited them on a desolate road. Each beggar held a tattered piece of tapestry in his hands.

**GO ON**

**12.** Where does this story take place?

   (F) in Japan

   (G) in China

   (H) in India

   (J) in Thailand

**13.** The widow supported her family by —

   (A) cutting wood.

   (B) selling weaving equipment.

   (C) weaving beautiful tapestries.

   (D) sewing clothes for rich people.

**14.** In this story, *painstaking* means —

   (F) causing intense pain.

   (G) great speed.

   (H) over and over again.

   (J) careful attention to detail.

**15.** By complaining about the time that their mother spent on the tapestry, Li Mo and Li Tu show that —

   (A) they are worried about their mother's health.

   (B) they are anxious to learn how to weave.

   (C) they are concerned only about themselves.

   (D) they dislike the tapestry.

**16.** Why did the widow work so long and hard on the new tapestry?

_____

_____

_____

_____

**17.** Li Mo and Li Tu were beggars because —

   (F) they could not find steady work.

   (G) they had been fired from their jobs.

   (H) they were sick and could not find work.

   (J) they had spent all their gold in the city and were too lazy to work.

**18.** In this story, the word *retrieve* means —

   (A) sell.

   (B) throw.

   (C) get back.

   (D) return.

**19.** Why were Li Mo and Li Tu swept by a ferocious windstorm?

   (F) They were being punished.

   (G) They were in the wrong place at the wrong time.

   (H) It was the windy season.

   (J) The fairy wanted them to go to Sun Mountain.

**20.** What lessons can be learned from this story?

_____

_____

_____

_____

_____

_____

_____

_____

_____

**GO ON**

# A Great American Patriot

Paul Revere was made famous by the poet Henry Wadsworth Longfellow in the poem "Paul Revere's Ride." Other details of Revere's life are less well-known, but probably as important to the effort to free the American colonies from British rule.

Revere was born in 1735 in Boston, Massachusetts, and was of French descent. His father was a silversmith, which is why Revere learned that trade while he also studied at Boston's North Grammar School.

Revere's work as the leader of the Boston craftworkers fired his interest in freedom for the American colonies. He worked alongside Samuel Adams and John Hancock—two revolutionary leaders. Revere was a *co-conspirator* in the Boston Tea Party. He created engravings of political cartoons in support of American liberty. He often delivered special messages to Boston patriots.

During the Revolutionary War, Paul Revere commanded a unit at Castle William in Boston Harbor. He later led the artillery division in a failed attempt to recapture control of land in Maine. *Accusations* of cowardice and disobedience were filed against Revere in connection with this failed attempt. He was found not guilty at his court-martial and later left the service.

Revere's other contributions to the Revolutionary War effort included the manufacture of gunpowder for the Continental Army, the designing and printing of the Continental currency, and the creation of the state seal that is still used by Massachusetts. In addition, Revere's knowledge of metal working was helpful when he made bronze cannons for the army.

Revere's silversmithing trade continued after the war. His silver tea sets are prized possessions for those fortunate enough to own them. He also cast bronze bells, which are still used in parts of New England today. His skill was put to good use when he made the copper fittings for the warship *U.S.S. Constitution*, also known as *Old Ironsides*.

> GO ON

Core Skills Test Prep, Grade 7

21. Why did Paul Revere learn the trade of silversmithing?

　Ⓐ　He learned the trade at Boston's North Grammar School.

　Ⓑ　He wanted to work with Samuel Adams.

　Ⓒ　His father was a silversmith.

　Ⓓ　He wanted to make copper fittings for warships.

22. What is the third paragraph *mainly* about?

　Ⓕ　Paul Revere's military career

　Ⓖ　Paul Revere's work in the American colonies' fight for freedom

　Ⓗ　Paul Revere's work as a silversmith

　Ⓙ　Paul Revere's education

23. In this selection, *co-conspirator* means —

　Ⓐ　one of many who were arrested.

　Ⓑ　a famous society person.

　Ⓒ　part owner.

　Ⓓ　one who secretly plots with others.

24. Which of Paul Revere's contributions to the Revolutionary War effort is the most famous?

　Ⓕ　the manufacture of gunpowder for the Continental Army

　Ⓖ　the design and printing of the Continental currency

　Ⓗ　his engravings of political cartoons

　Ⓙ　his ride to warn the American colonists that the British were coming

25. In this selection, the word *accusations* means —

　Ⓐ　formal charges.

　Ⓑ　proven lies.

　Ⓒ　military honors.

　Ⓓ　idle rumors.

26. There is enough information in this article to show that —

　Ⓕ　Paul Revere contributed in many ways to American freedom.

　Ⓖ　Paul Revere was the best soldier during the Revolutionary War.

　Ⓗ　Paul Revere was an excellent student at Boston's North Grammar School.

　Ⓙ　Paul Revere was a disappointing silversmith.

27. The web shows some ideas discussed in the selection.

```
                    Paul Revere
                   /           \
              Childhood       [         ]
              /      \          /        \
   born in   studied at   commanded   led an
   Boston    Boston's     a unit      artillery
             North                    division
             Grammar
             School
```

What word(s) would go in the empty box?

_____

_____

_____

_____

_____

_____

_____

© Houghton Mifflin Harcourt Publishing Company

**GO ON**

# SPEEDAWAY

The only name in bicycles. Our bicycles are the fastest ones on the road. That's why **SPEEDAWAY** is the bicycle brand you know and trust.

We make our bicycles with the customer in mind. Each bicycle is a SUPERIOR machine. You can't buy anything better. We guarantee that this bicycle will not be the CHEAPEST one you can buy. But we do guarantee that it is the best BRAND you can buy.

Our bicycles offer many special features. Here are some of them:

- 21-speeds

- Light-touch gear shifts for easy and accurate shifting

- Hand-pull caliper brakes

- 2-inch white side-wall tires

- Jelly-filled, cushioned seat

- 26-inch aluminum frame—This NEW and IMPROVED frame combines a reliably sturdy frame with the weight of a feather to produce a bicycle that literally flies down the road.

- 5-function electronic trip monitor that displays: speed, distance, average speed per mile, calories burned per mile, and length of time.

We truly believe in our bicycles. We are so sure you will like our bicycles that we will give you THREE FREE GIFTS—a safety helmet, a water bottle, and a pouch bag—when you purchase a **SPEEDAWAY** bicycle. If you are not satisfied with your bicycle, you may return it for your money back. BUT YOU GET TO KEEP THE FREE GIFTS!

Hurry on down to your local sporting goods store. If they don't have this bicycle, it's because they're sold out! Everyone carries our brand.

Buy **SPEEDAWAY**! You'll thank yourself for many years to come.

Core Skills Test Prep, Grade 7

**28.** Which of these is an *opinion* in the ad?

(A) You can't buy anything better…

(B) …electronic trip monitor that displays: speed, distance, …

(C) …you may return it for your money back…

(D) …you get to keep the free gifts…

**29.** All of these are features of the Speedaway bicycle *except* —

(F) 2-inch white-wall tires.

(G) a see-through plastic bug shield.

(H) hand-pull caliper brakes.

(J) a jelly-filled cushioned seat.

**30.** There is enough information in the ad to show that this product is —

(A) made in the United States.

(B) sold in most sporting goods stores.

(C) the poorest-selling bicycle in the country.

(D) used by most professional sports stars.

**31.** This ad was written mainly to tell about —

(F) the many products made by the manufacturers of the Speedaway brand bicycle.

(G) a new invention that is being sold.

(H) the many features of a brand-name bicycle.

(J) the stores where you can buy bicycles.

**32.** The ad tries to appeal to your desire to —

(A) buy a brand-name bicycle.

(B) have a bicycle like your best friend's bicycle.

(C) spend less money.

(D) look good.

**33.** The ad states that if you are not satisfied with the bicycle you may return it, get your money back, and keep the free gifts. Why do you think the company is making this offer?

_____

_____

_____

_____

_____

STOP

# Unit 10: Practice Test 2

## READING VOCABULARY

 You have 20 minutes to complete this test. Use the answer sheets on page 127 to mark your answers.

**Sample A**

Something that is <u>desolate</u> is —

(A) happy.

(B) bright.

(C) bleak.

(D) colorful.

**For questions 1–8, darken the circle for the word or group of words that has the same or almost the same meaning as the underlined word.**

1. <u>Sequence</u> means —
   (A) one at a time.
   (B) all at once.
   (C) in order.
   (D) as a group.

2. <u>Puny</u> means —
   (F) large.
   (G) significant.
   (H) tiny.
   (J) attractive.

3. To <u>confirm</u> is to —
   (A) believe.
   (B) contain.
   (C) choose.
   (D) prove.

4. To <u>attain</u> something is to —
   (F) lose it.
   (G) achieve it.
   (H) fail it.
   (J) confuse it.

5. A <u>cunning</u> person is —
   (A) popular.
   (B) sly.
   (C) educated.
   (D) well-known.

6. Someone who is <u>fashionable</u> is —
   (F) outdated.
   (G) clumsy.
   (H) crude.
   (J) stylish.

7. A <u>smirk</u> is a kind of —
   (A) smile.
   (B) cloth.
   (C) sound.
   (D) insult.

8. Something that is <u>severe</u> is —
   (F) weak.
   (G) harsh.
   (H) complete.
   (J) empty.

**GO ON**

## 105

Name _____ Date _____

**Sample B**

> Mom asked Tom to <u>load</u> the groceries into the car.

In which sentence does <u>load</u> have the same meaning as it does in the sentence above?

Ⓐ The mule carried a heavy <u>load</u>.

Ⓑ Her letter took a <u>load</u> off my mind.

Ⓒ Did you <u>load</u> the film into the camera?

Ⓓ We drove the <u>load</u> of potatoes to market.

_____

**For questions 9–13, darken the circle for the sentence in which the underlined word means the same as it does in the sentence in the box.**

9.

> The old prospector found a gold <u>mine</u>.

In which sentence does <u>mine</u> have the same meaning as it does in the sentence above?

Ⓐ The library is a <u>mine</u> of information.

Ⓑ Is this sweater yours or <u>mine</u>?

Ⓒ They own an agate <u>mine</u>.

Ⓓ Do they <u>mine</u> harbors with explosives?

10.

> I lost my ring near the tennis <u>net</u>.

In which sentence does <u>net</u> have the same meaning as it does in the sentence above?

Ⓐ She will <u>net</u> the fish.

Ⓑ The <u>net</u> weight of this box of cereal is 13 ounces.

Ⓒ Grandmother Lucy always wears a hair <u>net</u> to bed.

Ⓓ He hopes to <u>net</u> great profits from these investments.

11.

> The meteorologists will <u>track</u> the hurricane.

In which sentence does <u>track</u> have the same meaning as it does in the sentence above?

Ⓐ What animal made this <u>track</u>?

Ⓑ Jimmy was about to <u>track</u> mud on the new carpet.

Ⓒ I was able to <u>track</u> the injured animal into the woods.

Ⓓ Dr. Lee knows he's on the right <u>track</u> with his research.

12.

> The Mississippi River is a <u>major</u> waterway.

In which sentence does <u>major</u> have the same meaning as it does in the sentence above?

Ⓕ Is this symphony in a <u>major</u> key?

Ⓖ My uncle held the army rank of <u>major</u>.

Ⓗ I plan to <u>major</u> in science in college.

Ⓙ Suzanne spends the <u>major</u> part of her time studying.

13.

> Louisa will begin first <u>grade</u> in the fall.

In which sentence does <u>grade</u> have the same meaning as it does in the sentence above?

Ⓐ What is the highest <u>grade</u> of beef?

Ⓑ Kareem is now in the sixth <u>grade</u>.

Ⓒ I will try to <u>grade</u> all your papers tonight.

Ⓓ Renee has taken a <u>grade</u> six government job.

► **GO ON**

**106**

**Sample C**

We tried to <u>procure</u> enough supplies to last for five days. Procure means —

Ⓐ acquire.

Ⓑ pack.

Ⓒ find.

Ⓓ borrow.

**For questions 14–21, darken the circle for the word or words that give the meaning of the underlined word, or write in the answer.**

14. My throat was <u>parched</u> after three hours in the sun. Parched means —

Ⓕ sore.

Ⓖ red.

Ⓗ dry.

Ⓙ wet.

15. The expert says that bowl is <u>authentic</u> Wedgwood china. Authentic means —

Ⓐ ancient.

Ⓑ genuine.

Ⓒ false.

Ⓓ elegant.

16. Janet did not care for his <u>brash</u> manner. Brash means —

Ⓕ polite.

Ⓖ intelligent.

Ⓗ rude.

Ⓙ quiet.

17. The <u>flaw</u> in the fabric made it unusable. Flaw means —

_____

_____

_____

18. Many words are confusing because they have <u>multiple</u> meanings. Multiple means —

Ⓐ individual.

Ⓑ few.

Ⓒ long.

Ⓓ several.

19. The <u>horde</u> of aggressive reporters following the movie star was a big problem. Horde means —

Ⓕ small group.

Ⓖ crowd.

Ⓗ few.

Ⓙ individual.

20. Sandra said that she will <u>strive</u> to make the basketball team no matter how much work it takes. Strive means —

Ⓐ try.

Ⓑ ask.

Ⓒ quit.

Ⓓ rest.

21. Max was <u>flabbergasted</u> by the number of people who came to his birthday party. Flabbergasted means —

_____

_____

_____

**STOP**

**107**

# Unit 11: Practice Test 3

 You have 50 minutes to complete this test. Use the answer sheet on page 128 to mark your answers.

## PART 1: MATH PROBLEM SOLVING

**Sample A**

Which fraction is greater than $\frac{5}{8}$?

Ⓐ $\frac{2}{4}$  Ⓒ $\frac{3}{4}$

Ⓑ $\frac{2}{7}$  Ⓓ $\frac{3}{5}$

**For questions 1–47, darken the circle for the correct answer, or write in the answer.**

1. Which of the following decimals is greater than 0.273 and less than 0.291?

   Ⓐ 0.279
   Ⓑ 0.295
   Ⓒ 0.259
   Ⓓ 0.209

2. The number line shows 4 mice in a race. Which mouse is in the lead?

   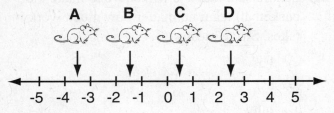

   Ⓕ mouse A
   Ⓖ mouse B
   Ⓗ mouse C
   Ⓙ mouse D

3. The temperature reading was −15°C at sunrise. By 3:00 P.M., the temperature had risen 20°. What was the temperature then?

   _____

   _____

4. At the candy store, 4 children each grabbed a handful of wrapped candy from the candy bin. The candy cost $1.49 per pound. The first child's handful of candy weighed $\frac{1}{3}$ pound. The second child's handful weighed $\frac{2}{5}$ pound, the third child's weighed $\frac{3}{10}$ pound, and the fourth's weighed $\frac{1}{4}$ pound. Which shows these amounts arranged in order from largest to smallest?

   Ⓐ $\frac{2}{5}, \frac{1}{3}, \frac{3}{10}, \frac{1}{4}$

   Ⓑ $\frac{3}{10}, \frac{1}{4}, \frac{2}{5}, \frac{1}{3}$

   Ⓒ $\frac{1}{4}, \frac{2}{5}, \frac{3}{10}, \frac{1}{3}$

   Ⓓ $\frac{1}{3}, \frac{2}{5}, \frac{1}{4}, \frac{3}{10}$

5. Which of these temperatures is colder than the temperature shown on the thermometer?

   Ⓕ −6°
   Ⓖ −2°
   Ⓗ 3°
   Ⓙ 0°

   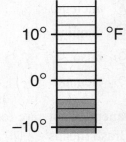

6. In the jet-engine racing car *Spirit of America*, a person can travel at 613.995 miles per hour. What is the value of the 5 in this number?

   Ⓐ 5 ten-thousandths
   Ⓑ 5 thousandths
   Ⓒ 5 hundredths
   Ⓓ 5 tenths

▶ **GO ON**

**7.** Madelynn lives 3 times as far from school as Liz does. If x is the number of blocks that Liz lives from school, which expression represents the distance Madelynn lives from school?

(F) $3x$

(G) $x - 3$

(H) $x + 3$

(J) $x/3$

**8.** Each ▱ represents 0.03.

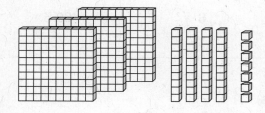

What decimal is shown by the figures above?

(A) 104

(B) 10.41

(C) 1.04

(D) 0.104

**9.** A special machine changes numbers according to a certain rule. The *out* number in the table shows the result when the rule is applied to the *in* number.

| In | 6 | 15 | 27 |
|---|---|---|---|
| Out | 2 | 5 | 9 |

What number will 24 be changed to?

_____

_____

_____

_____

_____

**10.** Dexter does volunteer work at a local retirement village. He wants to take some of the residents to a movie. The tickets cost $4.00 each. Dexter figures that it will cost $6.00 to drive his van to and from the movie theater. Which expression can Dexter use to find C, the total cost of the outing?

(F) $C = 4 + 6 + n$

(G) $6n - 4 = C + 6$

(H) $C = 4n + 6$

(J) $6(4n) = C$

**11.** The Richter Scale measures the magnitude of earthquakes and ranks them on a scale of 1 to 10. Each number on the scale stands for 30 times the magnitude of the number just before it. For example, if a reading on the Richter Scale is 2 more than another quake, it is $30^2$ times the magnitude. If an earthquake had a Richter Scale reading of 7, how would this be written to compare it to an earthquake with a Richter Scale reading of 2?

(A) $30^2$

(B) $30^3$

(C) $30^5$

(D) $30^7$

**12.** Look at the factor tree shown here.

Which numbers are missing from the factor tree?

(F) 2, 7

(G) 3, 6

(H) 4, 5

(J) 6, 9

**GO ON**

**13.** When 30 students were surveyed, 6 stated that they watch $2\frac{1}{2}$ hours of television each day. If 450 students were surveyed, how many students could be expected to watch $2\frac{1}{2}$ hours of television each day?

- Ⓐ  5
- Ⓑ  20
- Ⓒ  90
- Ⓓ  420

**14.** Cybil was making a design for art class by gluing beads to posterboard. She had 2 beads in the first row, 5 beads in the second row, 8 beads in the third row, and 11 beads in the fourth row. If this pattern continues, how many beads will she use in each of the next 3 rows?

- Ⓕ  22, 25, 28
- Ⓖ  12, 15, 18
- Ⓗ  15, 19, 23
- Ⓙ  14, 17, 20

**15.** If digits cannot be repeated, how many 3-digit numbers can be made using only the digits 3, 5, 6, 8, and 9?

- Ⓐ  5
- Ⓑ  24
- Ⓒ  36
- Ⓓ  60

**16.** What is another way to write $(4 \times 6) + (4 \times 4)$?

_____

_____

_____

_____

_____

**17.** Howard used an air pump to launch a model rocket. The table shows the number of pumps required to launch the rocket to specific heights. If it continued to operate at this rate, how many pumps would be required to launch the rocket to a height of at least 100 feet?

| Number of Pumps | Height in Feet |
| --- | --- |
| 3 | 40 |
| 4 | 47.5 |
| 5 | 55 |
| 6 | 62.5 |
| 7 | 70 |

- Ⓕ  12
- Ⓖ  11
- Ⓗ  10
- Ⓙ  8

**18.** Angela has 6 nickels and 8 pennies in her coin purse. What is the probability that Angela will randomly pick a nickel out of her coin purse?

- Ⓐ  $\frac{3}{7}$
- Ⓑ  $\frac{1}{8}$
- Ⓒ  $\frac{5}{5}$
- Ⓓ  $\frac{1}{2}$

**19.** In how many different ways can the letters in the word *MATH* be arranged?

_____

_____

_____

_____

_____

**GO ON**

**Use the graph to answer questions 20–22.**

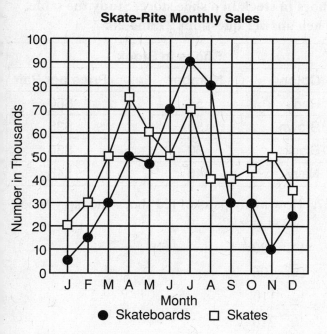

**Skate-Rite Monthly Sales**

● Skateboards  □ Skates

**20.** Which month on the graph shows the fewest sales of skateboards?

(F) January

(G) February

(H) September

(J) November

**21.** About how many more skates were sold in April than in November?

(A) 5,000

(B) 10,000

(C) 15,000

(D) 25,000

**22.** Describe the sale of skateboards between April and July.

_____

_____

_____

**In one week, a pet store made $1,000 in profits. The following graph shows the types of sales. Study the graph and answer questions 23 and 24.**

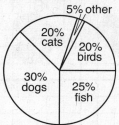

**PET STORE PROFITS**

5% other
20% cats
20% birds
30% dogs
25% fish

Total Profits = $1000

**23.** Which tally chart shows the data in the circle graph above?

(F)

| Cats | ℍℍ ℍℍ ℍℍ ℍℍ |
|------|------------------|
| Dogs | ℍℍ ℍℍ ℍℍ |
| Fish | ℍℍ ℍℍ ℍℍ ℍℍ |
| Birds | ℍℍ ℍℍ ℍℍ |
| Other | ℍℍ ℍℍ |

(G)

| Cats | ℍℍ ℍℍ |
|------|------------------|
| Dogs | ℍℍ ℍℍ ℍℍ |
| Fish | ℍℍ ℍℍ ℍℍ ℍℍ IIII |
| Birds | ℍℍ ℍℍ ℍℍ I |
| Other | ℍℍ ℍℍ II |

(H)

| Cats | ℍℍ ℍℍ ℍℍ ℍℍ |
|------|------------------|
| Dogs | ℍℍ ℍℍ ℍℍ ℍℍ ℍℍ ℍℍ |
| Fish | ℍℍ ℍℍ ℍℍ ℍℍ ℍℍ |
| Birds | ℍℍ ℍℍ ℍℍ ℍℍ |
| Other | ℍℍ |

(J)

| Cats | ℍℍ ℍℍ ℍℍ ℍℍ II |
|------|------------------|
| Dogs | ℍℍ ℍℍ ℍℍ II |
| Fish | ℍℍ ℍℍ ℍℍ ℍℍ ℍℍ I |
| Birds | ℍℍ ℍℍ ℍℍ III |
| Other | ℍℍ III |

**24.** How much more did the store make from sales of dogs than sales of cats?

_____

_____

_____

**GO ON**

**25.** Which transformation moves the figure from position A to position B?

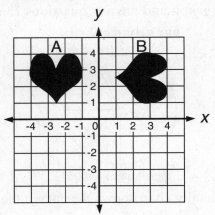

Ⓐ  extension

Ⓑ  rotation

Ⓒ  reflection

Ⓓ  translation

**26.** This bar graph shows Arnie's test scores in math class. What is his average (mean) score?

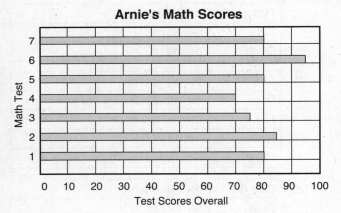

Ⓕ  85

Ⓖ  80

Ⓗ  75

Ⓙ  70

**This table shows the prices and the number of shoes in stock in a shoe store. Study the table. Then answer questions 27 and 28.**

| Shoes in Stock | | |
| --- | --- | --- |
| Color | Number | Price per Pair |
| Red | 54 | $50 |
| Brown | 50 | $35 |
| Black | 60 | $36 |
| Navy | 46 | $45 |

**27.** How many pairs of red shoes and navy shoes are in stock?

Ⓐ  100

Ⓑ  106

Ⓒ  110

Ⓓ  210

**28.** How much do 2 pairs of black shoes and 1 pair of navy shoes cost?

_____

_____

_____

**29.** The diameter of circle J is represented by which line segment?

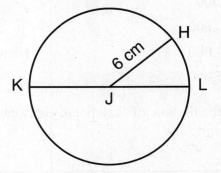

Ⓕ  $\overline{JH}$

Ⓖ  $\overline{JL}$

Ⓗ  $\overline{JK}$

Ⓙ  $\overline{KL}$

▶GO ON▶

Unit 11
Core Skills Test Prep, Grade 7

**30.** Which coordinates best represent the location of Banner on the map?

Ⓐ (4, 1)

Ⓑ (3, 2)

Ⓒ (2, 1)

Ⓓ (2, 3)

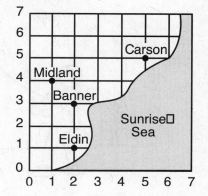

**31.** Which angle shown here is an acute angle?

Ⓕ  Ⓗ  Ⓖ  Ⓙ

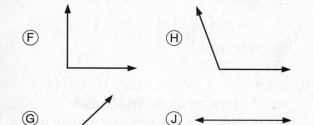

**Use the two triangles shown here to answer question 32.**

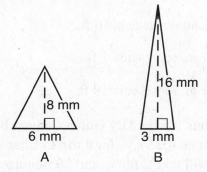

**32.** Which of the following statements about the two triangles is true?

Ⓐ Triangle A is smaller in area than Triangle B.

Ⓑ Both Triangle A and Triangle B have six angles that are right angles.

Ⓒ The area of Triangle A is one third larger than that of Triangle B.

Ⓓ The area of Triangle A is equal to the area of Triangle B.

**33.** If each cube shown here represents 1 cubic unit, what is the volume of this figure?

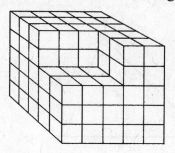

Ⓕ 125 cubic units

Ⓖ 113 cubic units

Ⓗ 105 cubic units

Ⓙ 25 cubic units

**34.** Each of the figures shown here can be folded to form a three-dimensional figure. Which can be folded to form a cube?

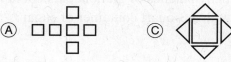

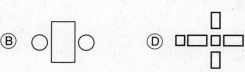

**35.** Which lines shown here are parallel?

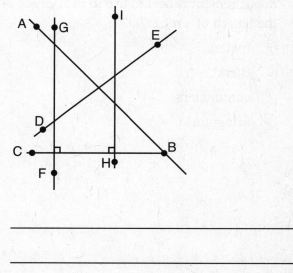

_____

_____

_____

▶GO ON

**113**

**36.** What is the area of triangle DFG?
(Use $A = \frac{1}{2} bh$.)

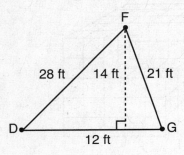

(F) 168 sq ft

(G) 84 sq ft

(H) 61 sq ft

(J) 49 sq ft

**37.** Larry wanted to bake granola bars for the club bake sale. Each batch took 1.5 cups of sugar. How many batches of granola bars could he make with a 3-quart container of sugar?

(A) 12

(B) 8

(C) 6

(D) 2

**38.** Which of the following metric units of measurement is best to use to measure the length of a room?

(F) meters

(G) liters

(H) centimeters

(J) kilograms

**39.** The picture shows that Toni is 10 yards from the tree. How many feet is that?

(A) 3 feet

(B) 30 feet

(C) 300 feet

(D) 3000 feet

**40.** For a history project, Jamie is making a scale drawing of the Washington Monument on a piece of posterboard that is $8\frac{1}{2}$ inches by 11 inches. If the monument is actually 555 feet high, what is a reasonable scale for her drawing?

(F) 1 in. represents 100 ft.

(G) 1 in. represents 10 ft.

(H) $\frac{1}{2}$ in. represents 1 ft.

(J) $\frac{1}{2}$ in. represents 10 ft.

**41.** The bus left the Dry Gulch Canyon bus station at 4:35 P.M. for a trip to Cherokee Flats that will take 2 hours and 50 minutes. At what time should the bus arrive at its destination?

_____

_____

_____

_____

_____

**GO ON**

**42.** The sum of the last two numerals in Max's apartment number is twice the sum of the first two numerals. Which of these could be Max's apartment number?

(A) 842

(B) 824

(C) 428

(D) 248

**43.** According to this table, about how much taller is the Willis Tower than the Empire State Building?

| World's Tallest Skyscrapers | |
|---|---|
| **Building** | **Height** |
| Amoco | 1,136 feet |
| Empire State Building | 1,250 feet |
| John Hancock Center | 1,127 feet |
| Willis Tower | 1,454 feet |

(F) 100 feet

(G) 150 feet

(H) 200 feet

(J) 300 feet

**44.** Which of the following units of measurement is best to use to describe the weight of a box of breakfast cereal?

(A) feet

(B) ounces

(C) liters

(D) inches

**45.** Marco took a box of popsicles to the park. He ate one and gave one to each of 5 friends. What do you need to know to find out how many popsicles Marco has left?

(F) how many friends chose grape popsicles

(G) how many popsicles altogether were in the box

(H) how many boxes of popsicles Marco ate at home

(J) how many orange popsicles were in the box

**46.** The cost of a pound of coffee is $3.69. The Martinez family buys 1.5 pounds of coffee each week. The Goldsmith family buys 2.5 pounds of coffee each week. Which question below cannot be answered using the data given above?

(A) What is the total weight of the coffee bought by the two families?

(B) What is the difference between the amount of coffee bought by the Martinez and Goldsmith families?

(C) How much coffee remains unused by each family at the end of the week?

(D) What would be the total cost of coffee bought by both families in one week?

**47.** Nora took swimming lessons before beginning piano lessons. She joined gymnastics class after beginning piano lessons. She began dance class before beginning swimming lessons. Which lessons did she begin first?

_____

_____

_____

STOP

**115**

# PART 2: MATH PROCEDURES

 You have 15 minutes to complete this test. Use the answer sheet on page 128 to mark your answers.

## Sample A

Mr. Rafael uses his own truck at work. If he drove 128 miles last week, and 62 of those miles were for his personal use, how many miles did he drive on the job?

- (A) 55 miles
- (B) 58 miles
- (C) 66 miles
- (D) 190 miles
- (E) NH

**STOP**

## Sample B

196
$\times$ 9

- (F) 954
- (G) 1,764
- (H) 1,954
- (J) 9,764
- (K) NH

**STOP**

**For questions 1–14, darken the circle for the correct answer. If the correct answer is not given, darken the circle for *NH, Not Here*. If no choices are given, write in the answer.**

**1.**

208
$\times$ 14

- (A) 2,812
- (B) 2,912
- (C) 2,922
- (D) 3,912
- (E) NH

**2.**

$33\overline{)1746}$

- (F) $22\frac{3}{11}$
- (G) 52
- (H) $52\frac{2}{11}$
- (J) $52\frac{10}{11}$
- (K) NH

**3.**

706
$\times$ 80

- (A) 56,480
- (B) 56,408
- (C) 56,068
- (D) 5,648
- (E) NH

**4.**

$12\frac{1}{8}$
$+ 4\frac{1}{4}$

- (F) $8\frac{1}{8}$
- (G) $16\frac{1}{6}$
- (H) $16\frac{3}{8}$
- (J) $16\frac{3}{16}$
- (K) NH

**5.**

$1.758 \times 3.6 =$

- (A) 0.63288
- (B) 6.3288
- (C) 63.288
- (D) 632.88
- (E) NH

**6.**

$\frac{5}{6} \div \frac{2}{9} =$

- (F) $3\frac{3}{4}$
- (G) $4\frac{3}{4}$
- (H) $\frac{5}{27}$
- (J) $5\frac{2}{7}$
- (K) NH

**7.**

$8\frac{7}{8} - 3\frac{5}{6} =$

- (A) $5\frac{1}{24}$
- (B) $5\frac{1}{8}$
- (C) $5\frac{3}{54}$
- (D) $5\frac{3}{16}$
- (E) NH

**8.**

$0.9\overline{)0.72}$

- (F) 8
- (G) 0.8
- (H) 0.08
- (J) 0.008
- (K) NH

**GO ON**

**9.** Tony brought a 132-ounce jug of a sports drink to football practice. If he wanted to share it equally with his 11 friends, how much would each person receive?

Ⓐ 11 ounces

Ⓑ 10 ounces

Ⓒ 8 ounces

Ⓓ 7 ounces

Ⓔ NH

**10.** A paper company has two factories that produce cardboard boxes. Factory A produces $2\frac{3}{4}$ million boxes a year and Factory B produces $4\frac{2}{3}$ million boxes a year. What is the total cardboard box production for the company in one year?

Ⓕ $7\frac{5}{12}$ million

Ⓖ $7\frac{7}{12}$ million

Ⓗ 8 million

Ⓙ $8\frac{2}{3}$ million

Ⓚ NH

**11.** Dominic bought 2 soccer balls for $39.45 each and a pair of soccer cleats for $44.99. Without including tax, how much did he spend altogether?

_____

_____

_____

_____

**12.** Danielle and 5 of her friends won 108 six-packs of juice drinks in a radio promotional contest. How many six-packs of drinks should Danielle receive as her $\frac{1}{6}$ share?

Ⓐ 11

Ⓑ 12

Ⓒ 16

Ⓓ 18

Ⓔ NH

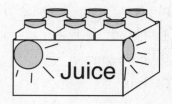

**13.** Marty tests water samples for the state park department. This morning he is preparing to test water from Lost Hollow Stream. How many $2\frac{1}{2}$-liter beakers can Marty fill with the 15 liters of water he has collected from the stream?

Ⓕ 12

Ⓖ 8

Ⓗ 6

Ⓙ 37.5

Ⓚ NH

**14.** Diane's craft club raised money by raffling a quilt the members had made. They raised $986 by selling tickets. The quilt cost $135 to make. How much profit did the club make?

_____

_____

_____

_____

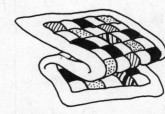

**STOP**

# Unit 12: Practice Test 4

 You have 25 minutes to complete this test. Use the answer sheets in the back of the book to mark your answers.

## LISTENING

**Sample A**

- Ⓐ avoid
- Ⓑ concentrate
- Ⓒ mix
- Ⓓ separate

**For questions 1–17, darken the circle for the word or words that best complete the sentence.**

1. Ⓐ completed
   Ⓑ late
   Ⓒ arrived
   Ⓓ recent

2. Ⓕ weak
   Ⓖ ill
   Ⓗ strong
   Ⓙ lonely

3. Ⓐ forgiven
   Ⓑ encouraged
   Ⓒ forbidden
   Ⓓ taxed

4. Ⓕ guard
   Ⓖ servant
   Ⓗ athlete
   Ⓙ clerk

5. Ⓐ speaker
   Ⓑ carpenter
   Ⓒ architect
   Ⓓ governor

6. Ⓕ an expert
   Ⓖ a specialist
   Ⓗ a veteran
   Ⓙ a beginner

7. Ⓐ welcome it
   Ⓑ ignore it
   Ⓒ follow it
   Ⓓ include it

8. Ⓕ following
   Ⓖ next
   Ⓗ previous
   Ⓙ effective

9. Ⓐ long
   Ⓑ crumbling
   Ⓒ winding
   Ⓓ straight

10. Ⓕ necessary
    Ⓖ unimportant
    Ⓗ optional
    Ⓙ intelligent

11. Ⓐ planning
    Ⓑ strength
    Ⓒ skill
    Ⓓ frailty

12. Ⓕ resist
    Ⓖ welcome
    Ⓗ deny
    Ⓙ acknowledge

13. Ⓐ soothed
    Ⓑ comforted
    Ⓒ bothered
    Ⓓ relieved

14. Ⓕ releasing
    Ⓖ enlisting
    Ⓗ rejecting
    Ⓙ training

15. Ⓐ false
    Ⓑ humorous
    Ⓒ truthful
    Ⓓ complete

16. Ⓕ different
    Ⓖ famous
    Ⓗ current
    Ⓙ beautiful

17. Ⓐ dread
    Ⓑ peace
    Ⓒ confidence
    Ⓓ trust

**GO ON**

Unit 12
Core Skills Test Prep, Grade 7

**Sample B**

A. gases from burning fuels that mix with rain

B. heavy rainfall

C. rain that falls on forests

D. rain that falls over farms

**STOP**

**For questions 18–30 darken the circle for the word or words that best answer the question.**

18. F. trees
    G. stones
    H. houses
    J. calendars

19. A. calendar
    B. village
    C. castle
    D. school

20. F. New York
    G. England
    H. Mexico
    J. Holland

21. A. "An Ancient Mystery"
    B. "Fun Vacation Spots"
    C. "Understanding Geology"
    D. "The English Calendar"

22. F. other countries
    G. shopping malls
    H. large cities
    J. cold climates

23. A. nacho
    B. caramel
    C. cheese
    D. butter

24. F. pierce the skins
    G. steam them first
    H. microwave them
    J. use a small amount of oil

25. A. placing them in a steamer
    B. baking them in an oven
    C. cooking them quickly over high heat
    D. microwaving them

26. F. "A Well-Balanced Diet"
    G. "Cooking Techniques for Vegetables"
    H. "Steaming Vegetables"
    J. "Vegetable Recipes"

27. A. a biology book
    B. a gardening book
    C. a plant book
    D. a cookbook

28. F. refreshments
    G. games
    H. contests
    J. music

29. A. in the auditorium
    B. in the school office
    C. in your classroom
    D. at a PTA meeting

30. F. on May 30th
    G. on the last day of school
    H. in the morning
    J. on April 30th

**STOP**

# Unit 13: Practice Test 5

You have 35 minutes to complete this test. Use the answer sheet on page 128 to mark your answers.

## LANGUAGE

### Sample A

Shari is planning to write a letter to her community library to request that the library purchase books about hot-air balloons. Before she writes the letter, she wants to find the titles of some books on the subject. She is currently reading the book *Ballooning*. To help her find the titles of other books on ballooning, she should look in this book's —

(A) title page.

(B) bibliography.

(C) index.

(D) dictionary.

**STOP**

**For questions 1–4, darken the circle for the correct answer, or write in the answer.**

In social studies class, Paul was assigned to write a report on some aspect of the history of transportation. He decided to research sailing ships and use this as the subject of his report.

1. What should Paul do before he writes his report?

(A) think of some famous sailing ships to include in his report

(B) reread his report for errors in sentence structure

(C) make a list of topics to include in his report

(D) check a dictionary for spellings of words to include in his report

2. What would Paul *not* want to include in his report?

(F) a chapter on ancient sailboats

(G) the development of steamships

(H) a discussion of the importance of the change from square to triangular sails

(J) a chapter on famous sailing ships

3. Where is the best place for Paul to find the most recent information about the design of modern sailing ships?

(A) a newspaper

(B) the *Readers' Guide to Periodical Literature*

(C) a telephone directory

(D) an encyclopedia

4. What method could Paul use to organize his thoughts before he writes his report?

_____

_____

**GO ON**

Here are the Table of Contents and the Index from books Paul found on the history of sailing ships. Read them carefully. Then answer questions 5–9.

## Book 1

### Table of Contents

## Book 2

### Index

**5.** Which pages in Book 2 would have information on the voyages of the Golden Hind?

_____

_____

**6.** Paul wanted to find information about explorers and the ships they used. All of these pages in Book 2 would be useful *except* —

- (F) 40
- (G) 42–45
- (H) 55
- (J) 28–30

**7.** Which chapter in Book 1 should Paul read to find the most information about the earliest kinds of sailing ships?

- (A) Chapter 1
- (B) Chapter 2
- (C) Chapter 3
- (D) Chapter 4

**8.** Which chapter in Book 1 should Paul read to find the most information about the ships used by Christopher Columbus when he landed in America?

- (F) Chapter 3
- (G) Chapter 4
- (H) Chapter 5
- (J) Chapter 6

**9.** Paul wanted to write a paragraph about a galleon used for fighting. On which pages in Book 2 could he probably find the most useful information on this topic?

_____

_____

_____

_____

_____

▶ GO ON ▶

**Here is a rough draft of the first part of Paul's report. Read the rough draft carefully. Then answer questions 10–16.**

## The History of Sailing Ships

The origin thousands of years ago, sailing ships date back to. Historians believe
**(1)**                                                                    **(2)**
that the earliest civilization to use sailing ships was that of the ancient Egyptians

The shape of the sail on the earliest sailing ships was square. A square-shaped
**(3)**                                                                    **(4)**
sail moved the earliest sailing ships. The mast, designed like a flagpole, held up
                                        **(5)**
the sail. Papyrus, a fibrous reedlike plant, grows plentifully along the Nile
        **(6)**
River. Besides being used to make a writing material, mats, and sandals,
        **(7)**
papyrus was used to make the earliest sails. Surprisingly, this early type of
                                        **(8)**
sailing ship is still used along the Nile in Egypt today. In the 1700s, most navies
                                        **(9)**
in the world were known as fleets.

As time passed, the Egyptians change in their sailing ships. They reworked
**(10)**                                                                   **(11)**
the mast so it was shaped like a long narrow A. The mast was secured to the
                                        **(12)**
ship with ropes. The boats by the crewmen who paddled them.
        **(13)**

**10.** Correctly rewrite sentence 1.

_____

_____

_____

_____

**11.** Which sentence needlessly repeats an idea?

Ⓐ 2
Ⓑ 3
Ⓒ 4
Ⓓ 5

**12.** Which of these sentences could be added after sentence 2?

Ⓕ The Egyptians used these ships to sail the Nile River.
Ⓖ The largest fighting ships, at this time, were made of iron.
Ⓗ By 1900 sailing ships were mostly used for pleasure or sport.
Ⓙ Why did people use sailing ships instead of steamboats?

**13.** Which sentence does *not* belong in paragraph 2? Write the number.

_____

_____

_____

_____

**14.** What is the best way to write sentence 10?

Ⓐ The Egyptians changed their sailing ships as time passed.
Ⓑ As time passed, the Egyptians changes in their sailing ships made.
Ⓒ As time passed, change in their sailing ships the Egyptians made.
Ⓓ As it is written.

**15.** Which of these sentences could be added after sentence 12?

Ⓕ Drawings of boats with sails have been found on early Egyptian pottery and on the walls of tombs.
Ⓖ Greek ships sailed everywhere in the Mediterranean world, from the Black Sea in the east to Spain in the west.
Ⓗ The ropes were lashed to the bow and to the stern of the ships.
Ⓙ The Egyptian ships were used to transport papyrus to the interior of Africa for trade.

**16.** Which group of words is *not* a complete sentence?

Ⓐ 9
Ⓑ 11
Ⓒ 12
Ⓓ 13

**GO ON**

Unit 13
Core Skills Test Prep, Grade 7

**Here is the next part of the rough draft of Paul's report. This part has certain words and phrases underlined. Read the draft carefully. Then answer questions 17–24.**

The phoenician civilization was also known for its sailing ships. The powerful
(14)                                                                (15)
Phoenicians were great sailors, traders navigators, and colonizers. They
(16)
controlled the trade on the Mediterranean Sea. They also had a large fleet of
(17)
sailing ships that were sturdy enough for the open seas of the Atlantic Ocean.

Phoenician ships had masts made from the timber of cedar trees and had
(18)
oars made of oak. In addition the boards for the hull were made from the timber
(19)
of fir trees. The hulls or frames of the sailing ships, were solidly built with ribs
(20)
for extra support. The front and back of the hull was sharp curved upward for
(21)
faster, smoother sailing. Linen cloth from Egypt was used for the sails.
(22)
Studying the construction of the earliest sailing ships makes people today
(23)
appreciate the skills of these early sailors. Anyone researching the history of
(24)
sailing ships were surprised at the seaworthiness of these early ships.

**7.** In sentence 14, <u>The phoenician civilization</u> is best written —

   Ⓕ  The Phoenician Civilization

   Ⓖ  The Phoenician civilization

   Ⓗ  the Phoenician civilization

   Ⓙ  As it is written.

**8.** In sentence 15, <u>sailors, traders navigators, and colonizers</u> is best written —

   Ⓐ  sailors, traders, navigators, and colonizers

   Ⓑ  sailors and traders, navigators, and colonizers

   Ⓒ  sailors and traders, and navigators and colonizers

   Ⓓ  As it is written.

**19.** In sentence 17, <u>They also had</u> is best written —

   Ⓕ  They also have

   Ⓖ  We also had

   Ⓗ  He and she also had

   Ⓙ  As it is written.

**20.** In sentence 19, <u>In addition the boards</u> is best written —

   Ⓐ  In addition the boards,

   Ⓑ  In addition, the boards,

   Ⓒ  In addition, the boards

   Ⓓ  As it is written.

**21.** In sentence 20, <u>hulls or frames of the sailing ships,</u> is best written —

   Ⓕ  hulls or frames of the sailing ships

   Ⓖ  hulls, or frames of the sailing ships,

   Ⓗ  hulls or frames, of the sailing ships

   Ⓙ  As it is written.

**22.** In sentence 21, <u>was sharp curved upward</u> is best written —

   Ⓐ  was sharp curve upward

   Ⓑ  was sharpest curve upward

   Ⓒ  were curved sharply upward

   Ⓓ  As it is written.

**23.** In sentence 23, <u>makes people today</u> is best written —

   Ⓕ  made people today

   Ⓖ  gives people today

   Ⓗ  has given people today

   Ⓙ  As it is written.

**24.** In sentence 24, <u>were surprised</u> is best written —

   Ⓐ  am surprised

   Ⓑ  will be surprised

   Ⓒ  will have been surprised

   Ⓓ  As it is written.

**GO ON**

**125**

**For questions 25–36, read each sentence carefully. If one of the words is misspelled, darken the circle for that word. If all the words are spelled correctly, then darken the circle for No mistake.**

25. She was <u>horse</u> from <u>cheering</u> after the team's big <u>victory</u>. <u>No mistake</u>
   (F)        (G)             (H)     (J)

26. I <u>dout</u> that the <u>package</u> will <u>arrive</u> today. <u>No mistake</u>
   (A)       (B)      (C)       (D)

27. Bill has <u>surffed</u> every <u>beach</u> on the northern <u>coast</u> of Hawaii. <u>No mistake</u>
   (F)       (G)       (H)       (J)

28. The actor's voice was <u>amplifyed</u> so he could be heard <u>throughout</u> the <u>theater</u>. <u>No mistake</u>
                                 (A)              (B)     (C)     (D)

29. The Department of <u>Commerce</u> <u>imposed</u> a new <u>tariff</u> on certain foreign imports. <u>No mistake</u>
                     (F)      (G)     (H)                     (J)

30. Her <u>house</u> is near the <u>intrasection</u> of Main Street and Willow <u>Avenue</u>. <u>No mistake</u>
       (A)            (B)                       (C)    (D)

31. We have had very <u>unpleasant</u> <u>whether</u> <u>lately</u>. <u>No mistake</u>
                  (F)        (G)    (H)    (J)

32. Muriel <u>wisked</u> the eggs well to make a <u>fluffy</u> <u>omelet</u>. <u>No mistake</u>
          (A)                  (B)    (C)     (D)

33. Most <u>historians</u> consider Athens the <u>birthplace</u> of <u>democratcy</u>. <u>No mistake</u>
         (F)                  (G)     (H)     (J)

34. The new budget <u>includes</u> a one-percent <u>increase</u> in sales <u>tacks</u>. <u>No mistake</u>
              (A)              (B)     (C)     (D)

35. My <u>physics</u> teacher <u>illustrated</u> her point by using a <u>transparentcy</u>. <u>No mistake</u>
       (F)       (G)              (H)     (J)

36. Juanita <u>practices</u> the <u>piano</u> for two hours every <u>afternoon</u>. <u>No mistake</u>
       (A)      (B)           (C)     (D)

**STOP**

# Answer Sheet for Students

| STUDENT'S NAME | | SCHOOL: |
|---|---|---|

**LAST**        **FIRST**    **MI**

TEACHER:

FEMALE ○      MALE ○

(Bubble grid for name: rows A–Z for each letter column)

## BIRTH DATE

| MONTH | | DAY | | YEAR | |
|---|---|---|---|---|---|
| Jan ○ | | ⓪ | ⓪ | ⓪ | ⓪ |
| Feb ○ | | ① | ① | ① | ① |
| Mar ○ | | ② | ② | ② | ② |
| Apr ○ | | ③ | ③ | ③ | ③ |
| May ○ | | | ④ | ④ | ④ |
| Jun ○ | | | ⑤ | ⑤ | ⑤ |
| Jul ○ | | | ⑥ | ⑥ | ⑥ |
| Aug ○ | | | ⑦ | ⑦ | ⑦ |
| Sep ○ | | | ⑧ | ⑧ | ⑧ |
| Oct ○ | | | ⑨ | ⑨ | ⑨ |
| Nov ○ | | | | | |
| Dec ○ | | | | | |

GRADE ④ ⑤ ⑥ ⑦ ⑧

### *Core Skills: Test Preparation* **Grade 7**

Fill in the circle for each multiple-choice answer. Write the answers to the open-ended questions on a separate sheet of paper.

## TEST 1     Reading Comprehension

SA Ⓐ Ⓑ Ⓒ Ⓓ    6. Ⓕ Ⓖ Ⓗ Ⓙ    12. Ⓕ Ⓖ Ⓗ Ⓙ    18. Ⓐ Ⓑ Ⓒ Ⓓ    24. Ⓕ Ⓖ Ⓗ Ⓙ    30. Ⓐ Ⓑ Ⓒ Ⓓ

1. Ⓐ Ⓑ Ⓒ Ⓓ    7. Ⓐ Ⓑ Ⓒ Ⓓ    13. Ⓐ Ⓑ Ⓒ Ⓓ    19. Ⓕ Ⓖ Ⓗ Ⓙ    25. Ⓐ Ⓑ Ⓒ Ⓓ    31. Ⓕ Ⓖ Ⓗ Ⓙ

2. Ⓕ Ⓖ Ⓗ Ⓙ    8. OPEN ENDED    14. Ⓕ Ⓖ Ⓗ Ⓙ    20. OPEN ENDED    26. Ⓕ Ⓖ Ⓗ Ⓙ    32. Ⓐ Ⓑ Ⓒ Ⓓ

3. Ⓐ Ⓑ Ⓒ Ⓓ    9. Ⓕ Ⓖ Ⓗ Ⓙ    15. Ⓐ Ⓑ Ⓒ Ⓓ    21. Ⓐ Ⓑ Ⓒ Ⓓ    27. OPEN ENDED    33. OPEN ENDED

4. Ⓕ Ⓖ Ⓗ Ⓙ    10. Ⓐ Ⓑ Ⓒ Ⓓ    16. OPEN ENDED    22. Ⓕ Ⓖ Ⓗ Ⓙ    28. Ⓐ Ⓑ Ⓒ Ⓓ

5. Ⓐ Ⓑ Ⓒ Ⓓ    11. OPEN ENDED    17. Ⓕ Ⓖ Ⓗ Ⓙ    23. Ⓐ Ⓑ Ⓒ Ⓓ    29. Ⓕ Ⓖ Ⓗ Ⓙ

## TEST 2     Reading Vocabulary

SA Ⓐ Ⓑ Ⓒ Ⓓ    4. Ⓕ Ⓖ Ⓗ Ⓙ    8. Ⓕ Ⓖ Ⓗ Ⓙ    11. Ⓐ Ⓑ Ⓒ Ⓓ    14. Ⓕ Ⓖ Ⓗ Ⓙ    18. Ⓐ Ⓑ Ⓒ Ⓓ

1. Ⓐ Ⓑ Ⓒ Ⓓ    5. Ⓐ Ⓑ Ⓒ Ⓓ    SB Ⓐ Ⓑ Ⓒ Ⓓ    12. Ⓕ Ⓖ Ⓗ Ⓙ    15. Ⓐ Ⓑ Ⓒ Ⓓ    19. Ⓕ Ⓖ Ⓗ Ⓙ

2. Ⓕ Ⓖ Ⓗ Ⓙ    6. Ⓕ Ⓖ Ⓗ Ⓙ    9. Ⓐ Ⓑ Ⓒ Ⓓ    13. Ⓐ Ⓑ Ⓒ Ⓓ    16. Ⓕ Ⓖ Ⓗ Ⓙ    20. Ⓐ Ⓑ Ⓒ Ⓓ

3. Ⓐ Ⓑ Ⓒ Ⓓ    7. Ⓐ Ⓑ Ⓒ Ⓓ    10. Ⓕ Ⓖ Ⓗ Ⓙ    SC Ⓐ Ⓑ Ⓒ Ⓓ    17. OPEN ENDED    21. OPEN ENDED

**127**

# Answer Sheet for Students (cont.)

## TEST 3     Part 1: Math Problem Solving

SA ⒶⒷⒸⒹ
1. ⒶⒷⒸⒹ
2. ⒻⒼⒽⒿ
3. OPEN ENDED
4. ⒶⒷⒸⒹ
5. ⒻⒼⒽⒿ
6. ⒶⒷⒸⒹ
7. ⒻⒼⒽⒿ
8. ⒶⒷⒸⒹ

9. OPEN ENDED
10. ⒻⒼⒽⒿ
11. ⒶⒷⒸⒹ
12. ⒻⒼⒽⒿ
13. ⒶⒷⒸⒹ
14. ⒻⒼⒽⒿ
15. ⒶⒷⒸⒹ
16. OPEN ENDED
17. ⒻⒼⒽⒿ

18. ⒶⒷⒸⒹ
19. OPEN ENDED
20. ⒻⒼⒽⒿ
21. ⒶⒷⒸⒹ
22. OPEN ENDED
23. ⒻⒼⒽⒿ
24. OPEN ENDED
25. ⒶⒷⒸⒹ
26. ⒻⒼⒽⒿ

27. ⒶⒷⒸⒹ
28. OPEN ENDED
29. ⒻⒼⒽⒿ
30. ⒶⒷⒸⒹ
31. ⒻⒼⒽⒿ
32. ⒶⒷⒸⒹ
33. ⒻⒼⒽⒿ
34. ⒶⒷⒸⒹ
35. OPEN ENDED

36. ⒻⒼⒽⒿ
37. ⒶⒷⒸⒹ
38. ⒻⒼⒽⒿ
39. ⒶⒷⒸⒹ
40. ⒻⒼⒽⒿ
41. OPEN ENDED
42. ⒶⒷⒸⒹ
43. ⒻⒼⒽⒿ
44. ⒶⒷⒸⒹ

45. ⒻⒼⒽⒿ
46. ⒶⒷⒸⒹ
47. OPEN ENDED

## TEST 3     Part 2: Math Procedures

SA ⒶⒷⒸⒹⒺ
SB ⒻⒼⒽⒿⓀ
1. ⒶⒷⒸⒹⒺ
2. ⒻⒼⒽⒿⓀ

3. ⒶⒷⒸⒹⒺ
4. ⒻⒼⒽⒿⓀ
5. ⒶⒷⒸⒹⒺ
6. ⒻⒼⒽⒿⓀ

7. ⒶⒷⒸⒹⒺ
8. ⒻⒼⒽⒿⓀ
9. ⒶⒷⒸⒹⒺ
10. ⒻⒼⒽⒿⓀ

11. OPEN ENDED
12. ⒶⒷⒸⒹⒺ
13. ⒻⒼⒽⒿⓀ
14. OPEN ENDED

## TEST 4     Listening

SA ⒶⒷⒸⒹ
1. ⒶⒷⒸⒹ
2. ⒻⒼⒽⒿ
3. ⒶⒷⒸⒹ
4. ⒻⒼⒽⒿ
5. ⒶⒷⒸⒹ

6. ⒻⒼⒽⒿ
7. ⒶⒷⒸⒹ
8. ⒻⒼⒽⒿ
9. ⒶⒷⒸⒹ
10. ⒻⒼⒽⒿ
11. ⒶⒷⒸⒹ

12. ⒻⒼⒽⒿ
13. ⒶⒷⒸⒹ
14. ⒻⒼⒽⒿ
15. ⒶⒷⒸⒹ
16. ⒻⒼⒽⒿ
17. ⒶⒷⒸⒹ

SB ⒶⒷⒸⒹ
18. ⒻⒼⒽⒿ
19. ⒶⒷⒸⒹ
20. ⒻⒼⒽⒿ
21. ⒶⒷⒸⒹ
22. ⒻⒼⒽⒿ

23. ⒶⒷⒸⒹ
24. ⒻⒼⒽⒿ
25. ⒶⒷⒸⒹ
26. ⒻⒼⒽⒿ
27. ⒶⒷⒸⒹ
28. ⒻⒼⒽⒿ

29. ⒶⒷⒸⒹ
30. ⒻⒼⒽⒿ

## TEST 5     Language

SA ⒶⒷⒸⒹ
1. ⒶⒷⒸⒹ
2. ⒻⒼⒽⒿ
3. ⒶⒷⒸⒹ
4. OPEN ENDED
5. OPEN ENDED
6. ⒻⒼⒽⒿ

7. ⒶⒷⒸⒹ
8. ⒻⒼⒽⒿ
9. OPEN ENDED
10. OPEN ENDED
11. ⒶⒷⒸⒹ
12. ⒻⒼⒽⒿ
13. OPEN ENDED

14. ⒶⒷⒸⒹ
15. ⒻⒼⒽⒿ
16. ⒶⒷⒸⒹ
17. ⒻⒼⒽⒿ
18. ⒶⒷⒸⒹ
19. ⒻⒼⒽⒿ
20. ⒶⒷⒸⒹ

21. ⒻⒼⒽⒿ
22. ⒶⒷⒸⒹ
23. ⒻⒼⒽⒿ
24. ⒶⒷⒸⒹ
25. ⒻⒼⒽⒿ
26. ⒶⒷⒸⒹ
27. ⒻⒼⒽⒿ

28. ⒶⒷⒸⒹ
29. ⒻⒼⒽⒿ
30. ⒶⒷⒸⒹ
31. ⒻⒼⒽⒿ
32. ⒶⒷⒸⒹ
33. ⒻⒼⒽⒿ
34. ⒶⒷⒸⒹ

35. ⒻⒼⒽⒿ
36. ⒶⒷⒸⒹ

Houghton Mifflin Harcourt Publishing Company

# Core Skills: Test Preparation, Grade 7

## ANSWER KEY

**Unit 2: Page 7**
1. C
2. F
3. looking back

**Page 8**
1. A
2. J
3. burns

**Page 9**
1. C
2. G
3. prizes or loot

**Page 10**
1. D
2. G
3. B
4. F

**Page 11**
1. A
2. J
3. The Chinese kung fu experts turned back the Japanese with their bare hands.

**Page 12**
1. A
2. H
3. The younger son left home after his father and brother disappeared.

**Page 13**
1. A
2. J
3. He went back to the post office.

**Page 14**
1. C
2. H
3. The volcano erupted during the fall.

**Page 15**
1. C
2. H
3. how trees can be protected from deer

**Page 16**
1. A
2. F
3. Wasps and bees have many differences.

**Pages 17–18**
1. B
2. G
3. B
4. H

**Page 19**
1. C
2. H
3. B
4. He had too much confidence.

**Page 20**
1. B
2. F
3. C
4. Sheila will probably go running.

**Pages 21–22**
1. A
2. May 13 would be the worst beach day because the temperature is low and the humidity is high.
3. F
4. The team's performance got worse for the 100m race.

**Page 23**
1. C
2. F
3. A
4. A nightmare awakened Charlene.

**Page 24**
1. A
2. H
3. D
4. Their problem got worse when they imported mongooses.

**Page 25**
1. C
2. J
3. A
4. Men and women have different habits.

**Page 26**
1. B
2. H
3. Bing's photos were mostly of people; Gilpin's photos were of scenery.
4. B
5. The women were tense and anxious.

**Pages 27–28**
1. C
2. H
3. Answers will vary.
4. D
5. J
6. 1. reduce toxins
   2. food decontamination
   3. longer shelf life

**Page 29**
1. B
2. J
3. D
4. F

**Pages 30–31**
1. B
2. J
3. D
4. G
5. D
6. Governments should spend more money to research edible plants.

**Unit 3: Pages 32–39**
Sample A: C
1. B
2. The school wants students to pack items and label boxes.
3. G
4. B
5. F
6. Nick's mood improved when spectators started clapping.
7. D
8. G
9. C
10. He said it would benefit their minds.
11. H
12. D
13. F
14. This notice would most likely be found in a school newsletter.
15. D
16. J
17. C
18. The author's purpose is to give information about an outdoor education program.
19. G
20. C
21. F
22. B
23. H
24. tennis court; wrist guards
25. Answers will vary.
26. C
27. H
28. by 1:00 on Sunday
29. C
30. J
31. You would most likely find this schedule in a local newspaper.

**Test, pages 40–48**
Sample A: C
1. D
2. F
3. The water is used to refill the car radiators when they boil over.
4. A
5. H
6. C
7. Answers will vary.
8. G
9. A
10. G
11. Answers will vary.
12. D
13. G
14. C
15. She became one of the 208 astronaut finalists.
16. H
17. B
18. G
19. Answers will vary.
20. C
21. J
22. C
23. H
24. The paintings on the wall in an Egyptian ruler's tomb show that he died from a bee sting.
25. B
26. F
27. B
28. The author wanted to inform readers about allergies.
29. G
30. A
31. G
32. C
33. F
34. She admires them for the way they treat their environment.
35. Jess decides to design a reusable bag for grocery stores.

**Unit 4: Page 49**
Sample A: B
1. C
2. G
3. A
4. J
5. D
6. F
7. C
8. H
9. D
10. F

**Page 50**
Sample A: A
1. D
2. H
3. B
4. H

**Page 51**
Sample A: B
1. C
2. G
3. A
4. loud or noisy
5. G
6. C
7. H
8. produce

**Test, pages 52–54**
Sample A: D
1. C
2. F
3. D
4. G
5. B
6. F
7. A
8. G
9. A
Sample B: D
10. G
11. C
12. G
13. A
14. Answers will vary.
Sample C: B
15. A
16. G
17. C
18. J
19. C
20. F
21. competent or efficient
22. noise

**Unit 5: Page 56**
**Step 1:** to determine the number of miles Justine drives to work in three weeks

**Step 2:** She drives 20 miles one way Monday through Thursday and 50 miles one way on Friday.

**Step 3:** Compute driving distance.

**Step 4:** 20 miles $\times$ 2 (for round trip) $\times$ 4 days = 160

50 miles $\times$ 2 (for round trip) $\times$ 1 day = 100

$$\begin{array}{r} 160 \\ +\ 100 \\ \hline 260 \text{ miles per week} \\ \times\ 3 \text{ weeks} \\ \hline 780 \text{ miles} \end{array}$$

**Step 5:** yes, because if the computations are correct,

780 miles is the number of miles she drove

**Page 57**

**Step 1:** to determine on which day he spent the most money

**Step 2:** On Monday, he spent $\frac{1}{2}$ of his $48. On Tuesday, he spent $\frac{1}{3}$ of the remainder. On Wednesday, he spent $\frac{1}{4}$ of the remainder. On Thursday, he spent $\frac{1}{6}$ of the remainder.

**Step 3:** Compare the numbers.

**Step 4:** On Monday, Ian spent the largest fraction of the largest amount. Therefore, it must be on Monday that he spent the greatest amount of money.

**Step 5:** yes, because the reasoning is sound

**Unit 6: Page 58**
Sample A: A
1. C
2. F
3. A
4. 5°

**Page 59**
Sample A: C
1. B
2. H
3. C
4. 2

**Page 60**
Sample A: B
1. C
2. J
3. A
4. J
5. $46.50

**Page 61**
Sample A: A
1. D
2. 20
3. H
4. B

**Pages 62–63**
Sample A: B
1. B
2. 188
3. J
4. C
5. F
6. B
7. F

8. B
9. $780

**Pages 64–65**
Sample A: D
1. A
2. 600 sq ft
3. H
4. B
5. F
6. C
7. J
8. D
9. radius

**Pages 66–67**
Sample A: C
1. D
2. H
3. 4 inches
4. D
5. H
6. B
7. F
8. D
9. 18 feet
10. 45 minutes

**Page 68**
Sample A: C
1. D
2. 30 cars
3. G
4. 42 44 46 48 50 52

**Page 69**
Sample A: B
1. D
2. H
3. C
4. G
5. 3,000 miles

**Page 70**
Sample A: C
1. E
2. G
3. A
4. F
5. B
6. J

**Page 71**
Sample A: C
1. A
2. H
3. C
4. H

**Test 1, pages 72–77**
Sample A: C
1. B
2. G
3. A
4. H
5. C
6. G
7. All are multiples of 3.
8. C
9. J
10. 40
11. B

12. J
13. D
14. F
15. C
16. F
17. narrow tip
18. B
19. J
20. C
21. H
22. F
23. H
24. $\overline{AC}$
25. D
26. G
27. D
28. H
29. 8:09 a.m.
30. C
31. J
32. 12
33. B
34. 50
35. H
36. C
37. J
38. A

**Test 2, pages 78–79**
Sample A: E
Sample B: H
1. B
2. F
3. A
4. H
5. A
6. H
7. C
8. 201,210
9. H
10. C
11. F
12. D
13. H
14. $2.34

**Unit 7: Page 80**
Sample A: C
1. C
2. G
3. D
4. F
5. D
6. F
7. C
8. H
9. D
10. courageous, heroic or brave

**Page 81**
Sample A: A
1. A
2. G
3. D
4. G
5. A
6. H
7. D
8. G
9. A
10. G

**Test, pages 82–83**
Sample A: C
1. B
2. H
3. D
4. G
5. D
6. G
7. A
8. H
9. A
10. J
11. B
12. F
13. undamaged
Sample B: B
14. B
15. H
16. A
17. F
18. A
19. F
20. B
21. G
22. B
23. J
24. A
25. J
26. "Our Summer Jobs"

**Unit 8: Pages 84–89**
Sample A: B
1. C
2. G
3. D
4. F
5. A
6. Chapter 6
7. H
8. A
9. G
10. D
11. J
12. The coral remains in this home for life.
13. D
14. G
15. A
16. Lagoons, shallow ponds with no place to hide, are dangerous places for colorful fish.
17. G
18. C
19. H
20. It protects itself from predators by using poison.

**Page 90**
Sample A: C
1. D
2. G
3. A
4. G
5. A
6. G

7. A
8. F

**Test, pages 91–95**
Sample A: C
1. D
2. He wants to learn more about the Olympic Games.
3. G
4. A
5. H
6. 10
7. A
8. G
9. their
10. A
11. J
12. C
13. G
14. B
15. H
16. B
17. H
18. D
19. F
20. B
21. F
22. A
23. J
24. C

**Pages 96–126**
See pages 131 and 132 for the multiple-choice answers.

**Comprehensive Tests: Open-Ended Answers**

**Page 98**
8. Answers will vary.
11. PETE

**Page 100**
16. It was a picture of everything she dreamed of and cherished.
20. Devotion and kindness are rewarded; selfishness and greed are punished.

**Page 102**
27. Army Service

**Page 104**
33. Sample answer: to show that the company really believes in its bicycle

**Page 107**
17. defect
21. astonished

**Page 108**
3. 5°

**Page 109**
9. 8

**Page 110**
16. $4 \times 10$ or $4(6 + 4)$
19. 24

**Page 111**
22. Sales dropped slightly, then rose sharply.
24. $100

**Page 112**
28. $117

**Page 113**
35. $\overline{GF}$ and $\overline{IH}$

**Page 114**
41. 7:25 p.m.

**Page 115**
47. dance lessons

**Page 117**
11. $123.89
14. $851

**Page 120**
4. Make a concept web showing the history of sailing ships.

**Page 121**
5. 70 and 72
9. 61–64

**Page 123**
10. The origin of sailing dates back thousands of years.
13. 9

Houghton Mifflin Harcourt Publishing Company

# Answer Sheet for Students

**STUDENT'S NAME**

**LAST**      **FIRST**    **MI**

**SCHOOL:**
**TEACHER:**
**FEMALE** ○    **MALE** ○

**ANSWER KEY**

| BIRTH DATE | | |
|---|---|---|
| **MONTH** | **DAY** | **YEAR** |
| Jan ○ | ⓪ ⓪ | ⓪ ⓪ |
| Feb ○ | ① ① | ① ① |
| Mar ○ | ② ② | ② ② |
| Apr ○ | ③ ③ | ③ ③ |
| May ○ | ④ | ④ ④ |
| Jun ○ | ⑤ | ⑤ ⑤ |
| Jul ○ | ⑥ | ⑥ ⑥ |
| Aug ○ | ⑦ | ⑦ ⑦ |
| Sep ○ | ⑧ | ⑧ ⑧ |
| Oct ○ | ⑨ | ⑨ ⑨ |
| Nov ○ | | |
| Dec ○ | | |

**GRADE** ④ ⑤ ⑥ ⑦ ⑧

*Core Skills:*
*Test Preparation*
## Grade 7

Fill in the circle for each multiple-choice answer. Write the answers to the open-ended questions on a separate sheet of paper.

## TEST 1    Reading Comprehension

| | | | | | |
|---|---|---|---|---|---|
| SA (A) (B) (C) **D** | 6. **F** (G) (H) (J) | 12. (F) **G** (H) (J) | 18. (A) (B) **C** (D) | 24. (F) (G) (H) **J** | 30. (A) (B) (C) **D** |
| 1. (A) (B) **C** (D) | 7. **A** (B) (C) (D) | 13. (A) (B) **C** (D) | 19. **F** (G) (H) (J) | 25. **A** (B) (C) (D) | 31. (F) (G) **H** (J) |
| 2. **F** (G) (H) (J) | 8. OPEN ENDED | 14. (F) (G) (H) **J** | 20. OPEN ENDED | 26. **F** (G) (H) (J) | 32. **A** (B) (C) (D) |
| 3. (A) **B** (C) (D) | 9. **F** (G) (H) (J) | 15. (A) (B) **C** (D) | 21. (A) (B) **C** (D) | 27. OPEN ENDED | 33. OPEN ENDED |
| 4. (F) (G) **H** (J) | 10. **A** (B) (C) (D) | 16. OPEN ENDED | 22. (F) **G** (H) (J) | 28. **A** (B) (C) (D) | |
| 5. (A) (B) **C** (D) | 11. OPEN ENDED | 17. (F) (G) (H) **J** | 23. (A) (B) (C) **D** | 29. (F) **G** (H) (J) | |

## TEST 2    Reading Vocabulary

| | | | | | |
|---|---|---|---|---|---|
| SA (A) (B) **C** (D) | 4. (F) **G** (H) (J) | 8. (F) (G) **H** (J) | 11. (A) (B) **C** (D) | 14. (F) (G) **H** (J) | 18. (A) (B) (C) **D** |
| 1. (A) (B) **C** (D) | 5. (A) **B** (C) (D) | SB **A** (B) (C) (D) | 12. (F) (G) (H) **J** | 15. (A) (B) **C** (D) | 19. (F) **G** (H) (J) |
| 2. (F) (G) **H** (J) | 6. (F) (G) (H) **J** | 9. (A) (B) **C** (D) | 13. (A) **B** (C) (D) | 16. (F) (G) **H** (J) | 20. **A** (B) (C) (D) |
| 3. (A) (B) (C) **D** | 7. **A** (B) (C) (D) | 10. **F** (G) (H) (J) | SC **A** (B) (C) (D) | 17. OPEN ENDED | 21. OPEN ENDED |

**131**

© Houghton Mifflin Harcourt Publishing Company

**Answer Key**
Core Skills Test Prep, Grade 7

# Answer Sheet for Students (cont.)

## TEST 3    Part 1: Math Problem Solving

| SA. **C** | 9. Open Ended | 18. **A** | 27. **A** | 36. **H** | 45. **G** |
|---|---|---|---|---|---|
| 1. **A** | 10. **H** | 19. Open Ended | 28. Open Ended | 37. **B** | 46. **C** |
| 2. **J** | 11. **C** | 20. **F** | 29. **J** | 38. **F** | 47. Open Ended |
| 3. Open Ended | 12. **H** | 21. **D** | 30. **B** | 39. **B** | |
| 4. **A** | 13. **C** | 22. Open Ended | 31. **G** | 40. **F** | |
| 5. **F** | 14. **H** | 23. **H** | 32. **C** | 41. Open Ended | |
| 6. **A** | 15. **C** | 24. Open Ended | 33. **G** | 42. **D** | |
| 7. **F** | 16. Open Ended | 25. **B** | 34. **A** | 43. **H** | |
| 8. **A** | 17. **G** | 26. **G** | 35. Open Ended | 44. **C** | |

## TEST 3    Part 2: Math Procedures

| SA. **C** | 3. **A** | 7. **A** | 11. Open Ended |
|---|---|---|---|
| SB. **G** | 4. **G** | 8. **G** | 12. **D** |
| 1. **B** | 5. **B** | 9. **A** | 13. **H** |
| 2. **J** | 6. **F** | 10. **F** | 14. Open Ended |

## TEST 4    Listening

| SA. **C** | 6. **J** | 12. **J** | SB. **A** | 23. **B** | 29. **B** |
|---|---|---|---|---|---|
| 1. **B** | 7. **D** | 13. **C** | 18. **G** | 24. **F** | 30. **F** |
| 2. **H** | 8. **H** | 14. **G** | 19. **A** | 25. **C** | |
| 3. **C** | 9. **C** | 15. **B** | 20. **G** | 26. **G** | |
| 4. **F** | 10. **F** | 16. **H** | 21. **A** | 27. **D** | |
| 5. **A** | 11. **A** | 17. **B** | 22. **H** | 28. **H** | |

## TEST 5    Language

| SA. **A** | 7. **A** | 14. **D** | 21. **G** | 28. **B** | 35. **H** |
|---|---|---|---|---|---|
| 1. **C** | 8. **H** | 15. **H** | 22. **C** | 29. **J** | 36. **D** |
| 2. **G** | 9. Open Ended | 16. **D** | 23. **J** | 30. **B** | |
| 3. **B** | 10. Open Ended | 17. **H** | 24. **A** | 31. **G** | |
| 4. Open Ended | 11. **C** | 18. **B** | 25. **F** | 32. **A** | |
| 5. Open Ended | 12. **F** | 19. **J** | 26. **A** | 33. **G** | |
| 6. **J** | 13. Open Ended | 20. **C** | 27. **F** | 34. **C** | |

# ANSWER KEY

132